Belleville
the good old days

Belleville
THE GOOD OLD DAYS

Compiled by
NICK AND HELMA MIKA

MIKA PUBLISHING COMPANY
Belleville, Ontario
1975

Belleville, looking East, 1830's, showing the lower bridge.

Belleville, The Good Old Days
Copyright © Mika Publishing Company, 1975
ISBN 0-919302-98-X
Printed and bound in Canada

Contents

Bank of Montreal, built 1856, Victoria Avenue and Pinnacle Street.

Acknowledgements

Our sincere appreciation goes to Dr. Gerald Morton and Mr. Myles Morton of *The Intelligencer* who permitted us to make use of their archives and glean some of the stories which were recorded on the pages of the Belleville paper over the past one hundred years. We also wish to say thank you to the writers who contributed the articles telling of Belleville's "good old days".

Introduction

by

Gerald E. Boyce

This volume could not have happened twenty years ago. At that time most Canadians took so little interest in their country's past that books on local history were few and far between. Earlier, when W. C. Mikel published a history of Belleville in 1943, he found it impossible to sell all five hundred copies. By contrast, in 1975 when Mika Publishing Company brought out a history of the small community of Wooler, the first printing of seven hundred copies was sold out in short order.

The 1967 celebration of the Centennial of Canadian Confederation had a great impact on Canadians' attitudes towards their history. Our attention was focused dramatically on the fact that we had a heritage of which we could be proud, a history that was in no way inferior to that of other nations. Accordingly, many Canadians were prepared to take a fresh look at the history of their local communities.

This growing awareness of community history was accompanied by an increase in the number of published local histories. Leading the way in this activity were Nick and Helma Mika, whose *Mosaic of Belleville* (1966) ushered in a series of original and reprinted volumes dealing with Canadian history — especially at the local level. Among these later books was the Mikas *Belleville, Friendly City* (1973), a portrait of Belleville's past and present.

These volumes (together with others such as *Historic Hastings* published by Hastings County Council in 1967) have done much to encourage the study of local history in our schools. For example, at Centennial and Moira secondary schools, grade nine pupils are introduced to historical research by examining the books, manuscripts, maps, pictures, and other records of Hastings and Prince Edward counties.

The approaching celebration of Belleville's Centennial as a city (1878-1978) has encouraged the Mikas to issue this volume. They have collected the work of several well-known local writers to illustrate some of the interesting and unusual aspects of Belleville's history. It is my hope that public acceptance of this book will encourage the Mikas to publish further volumes on Belleville before Centennial '78.

View of Belleville in the 1830's, sketched by Thomas Burrowes. The long building with two doors on the east bank of the river was the Wallbridge residence, formerly the Simpson inn, on the northeast corner of Front and Dundas Streets.

Historic Belleville: A Thumbnail Sketch

by Gerald E. Boyce

The site of the present city of Belleville has been settled for many years. Among the earliest inhabitants (according to Wallace Havelock Robb) were the far Keepers of the Flint, a Mohawk tribe whose village of Kente moved hither and yon in the Quinte area. In his Canadian epic "Thunderbird", Robb, a native of Belleville and a prominent Canadian poet, suggested that Kente was located for a time at the mouth of the river which the earlier Algonquin tribes had named Sagonaska. The translation of the name Sagonaska suggests "Where the waves of the river dance with the waves of the bay — scintillating waves — disturbed currents". The present generation knows this river as the Moira.

To the early French explorers, the Moira was "R. du Barbu" (Catfish River) and catfish still may be found in its waters.

The first white man known to have passed this way was the noted French explorer Samuel de Champlain, but whether he actually visited or even saw this site is uncertain. What is known is that in 1615 Champlain passed down the neighbouring Trent River and crossed over the Bay of Quinte, with a Huron war party on its way to attack an Iroquois village on the south shore of Lake Ontario, near Oswego.

The first white settlement in the vicinity of Belleville was an Indian mission to the Cayugas. Believed to have been located in the Consecon area south of Trenton, this mission was established by Fathers Trouvé and Fenelon of the Sulpician Order. This mission, known as the Kente or Quinte Mission survived from 1668 until 1682, when the cost of maintaining the venture (coupled with its lack of success) forced its abandonment.

The American Revolution (or War of Independence—as—our American friends call it) was a boon to the white settlement of our area. Following the defeat of the British forces and their provincial allies, a number of United Empire Loyalists settled in what is now the province of Ontario. Many of the women and children came from the refugee camps near Montreal where they had lived for several years while their menfolk served in the provincial regiments. Other Loyalists came directly from the Thirteen Colonies.

Simpson's Tavern.

The arrival of the Loyalists meant the introduction of English laws, religion, and culture to this region, which hitherto had been governed as a part of French-speaking Quebec. The first surveyed lands in the Quinte area, originally planned as seigneuries to fit in with the seigneurial system of landholding in Quebec, were instead proclaimed as townships and the English system of freehold tenure was introduced. These lands were granted to the Loyalists and the front sections along the Bay of Quinte began to fill up, commencing in 1784.

Among the first settlers at the site of Belleville was Captain George Singleton, a Loyalist with a distinguished record in the King's Royal Regiment of New York. [He is less highly regarded in New York State, where even today he is remembered in local histories as the villain who allegedly ordered his Indian allies to kill their Revolutionary prisoners.] At the mouth of the Moira, Singleton conducted a profitable trading business for several years after 1785, until his untimely death in 1789. During this period, the river was called Singleton's Creek and the small settlement near its mouth was known as Singleton's.

Part of Captain Meyers' mill, erected in 1790's.

After Singleton's death, his place as the community's leading merchant was taken by Captain John W. Meyers. He established Belleville's first industries — a sawmill and a gristmill — and engaged in a flourishing trading business. As a result the small community was known as Meyers' Creek in his honour.

The arrival of trade rivals and a suspicion that Meyers had not been as devoted to the British and Canadian cause in the War of 1812-14 as he might have been, prompted a change in name in 1816. At that time, the village's population had reached one hundred and fifty and there were some fifty homes, stables, taverns, and other buildings. A settlement of that size seemed to merit an official name, and so a gathering of prominent citizens in Simpson's Tavern decided upon the name "Bellville." This was said to be in honour of Lady Arabella Gore, wife of provincial lieutenant-governor Sir Francis Gore. Nonetheless, over the years there have been some authorities who see the name "Bellville" as perhaps owing something to merchant and schoolteacher William Bell, a commercial rival of Captain Meyers.

The settlement's early growth was slow, but the demand in England for timber and the rich forests that were easily accessible by the Moira River soon led to a boom. Belleville became a bustling lumber town and many stories are told of the very colourful French-Canadian loggers bringing the logs down the river to the waiting sawmills. At Belleville, the logs were either cut into timber at the several mills (some of which employed a hundred men and loaded a schooner every twenty-four hours) or were rafted and taken down the St. Lawrence to Quebec.

While the lumber boom continued, prosperity was at a peak. Moreover, the arrival of the Grand Trunk Railway in 1856 gave Belleville a rail link with Montreal and Toronto; Belleville was a division point on the line and the railway for many years was the town's largest employer. Industries developed rapidly and local agricultural implement factories and foundries found a wide market for their products throughout eastern Canada. The discovery of gold near Madoc in 1866 led to Belleville being known as the Gateway to the Golden North, although this name soon fell into disuse when the mines did not live up to their promoters' expectations.

In 1857, encouraged by the recent arrival of the Grand Trunk Railway and the expansion of local industry and agriculture, the citizens of Belleville petitioned Queen Victoria to name this city as the capital of Canada. Unfortunately, the petition was misdirected and this factor — coupled with other considerations such as the need for a capital city closer to French Canada and farther from possible American aggression — led to the honour not being granted. Ottawa was selected.

Belleville has been described as a bustling and perhaps somewhat vulgar lumber town in the mid-nineteenth century, and so it was. It was also a centre of culture and society. A visitor in 1834 noted that "The children as well as the ladies are most beautifully dressed in silks with their veils and parasols." In 1857, Albert College was set up as a Methodist College; it joined the district grammar school as an elevating influence.

Indicative of the development of the town was the erection of such attractive stone buildings as the former Hastings County Court House and Gaol in 1838. This handsome building, demolished after 1960 to make way for the new County Administration Building, dominated the landscape of the town for more than a century. Among the first officials to serve in the Court House was Dunbar Moodie, a writer of some talent himself and the husband of noted authoress Susanna Moodie. Mrs. Moodie's best known works are *Roughing it in the Bush* and *Life in the Clearings*, the latter painting a vivid picture of life in Belleville in the 1840's. For many years the Moodies lived in the stone cottage which still stands at the corner of West Bridge and Sinclair streets.

The terraced lawn in front of the original Court House was the scene of many impressive ceremonies, among them the local celebration of Canadian Confederation on July 1, 1867. But the cannon on the Court House lawn that announced the dawn of a new era for British North America was the herald of recession and depression for this town. Although the town officially became a city in 1878, the lumber trade was in serious decline by that date, industry largely remained at a standstill, and the community's population increased very little from 1875 to 1900.

Only with the Twentieth Century has Belleville resumed its growth. New industries have located here and the city has grown both in size and prosperity. Perhaps more important, the quality of life has improved.

How Belleville was Named

by Nick and Helma Mika

The City of Belleville is situated on the northern shore of the Bay of Quinte, at the mouth of the River Moira in the southwest corner of the Township of Thurlow, and in the County of Hastings.

The spot at present occupied by the city appears to have been the site of an Indian village in very early times. The village, however, was a mere collection of wigwams, which shifted their positions several times in the course of the year, to suit the fancy or convenience of the inhabitants. The greater part of the land in the neighbourhood was a desolate cedar swamp.

The Mississauga Indians called this place "Asaukhknosk", or in our language, "the place where the rushes end". The river which enters the Bay of Quinte here was known as "Saganaska".

In 1784, Captain George Singleton, a United Empire Loyalist, and his brother-in-law, Lieutenant Israel Ferguson, settled in the immediate vicinity. Captain Singleton opened a trading post on the east side of the Moira River. The small settlement was known as "Singleton's Creek", and the river was known as Singleton's River.

Both Singleton and Ferguson died within a short time of each other during the year of 1789. In the same year the first main group of settlers arrived in the vicinity of Belleville. Among these settlers were John Taylor who purchased one hundred acres of Captain Singleton's property, and John Simpson who built the first tavern, which stood until 1870 at the intersection of Dundas and Front Streets. This tavern soon became the social centre in the area.

The first cluster of houses began to form on the east side of the river, near its confluence with the bay. The earliest building erected on this site is believed to have been a small log cabin built by Asa Wallbridge, a fur trader.

Simpson's Tavern, erected in the 1800's. Later it was sold to the Wallbridge family.
This was the place where Belleville was named.

Early in the year 1790, Captain John Walden Meyers (also found spelled John Waltermeyer), a gentleman who had fought valiantly on the Royal side during the War of the Revolution, purchased from John Taylor the rear half of the land purchased by the latter from Captain Singleton. Meyers built a log house on the east bank of the river, erected a dam, and built a lumber mill and and a grist mill.

The river on which Captain Meyers had built his mills came to be known as "Meyers' Creek", and the name was also applied to the settlement at the river's mouth. Hard working, resourceful and bold, Captain Meyers soon expanded his activities to include a trading post and a distillery. He played a vital part in the development of the settlement. Being the first to harness the water power and establish an industry at the site, he is considered the founder of Belleville.

On the west side of the river, shortly after 1800, two Scotchmen, Simon and James McNabb, had purchased land from Alexander Chisholm and had built a dam, a flouring mill and a small cloth factory, just below Captain Meyers' establishment. Ambitious men, both officers in the militia, the two brothers soon made their influence felt in the village, rivalling Captain Meyers' in business and politics.

KINGSTON, AUGUST 24, 1816.

. . . .

THE Lieut. Governor, in Council, has been pleased to give the New Town, (formerly distinguished by the name of "*Myers' Creek*,") at the River Moira, the name of "BELLEVILLE," by the request and petition of a great number of the inhabitants of that town, and the township of Thurlow.

Notice in the *Kingston Gazette*, August 24, 1816: Naming of Belleville.

The substantial influence Captain Meyers had wielded was dealt a severe blow during the War of 1812. He was accused of not aiding in the war effort and was said to have deserted a wagon-load of supplies, which he was supposed to drive to York (Toronto), by unhitching his team at Brighton and returning to Meyers' Creek. James McNabb brought these charges before the provincial government in 1815 and requested that no honours should be bestowed on Captain Meyers in the future. Thus it came about that "Meyers' Creek" was not chosen as a permanent name for the settlement.

The final blow came in 1816, when Lieutenant-Governor Francis Gore stopped at Meyers' Creek on his way to York. With him was travelling his young and beautiful wife, Lady Bella Gore. It was as a result of this visit that the McNabb brothers and their friends decided to name the village after Lady Bella Gore.

The event was described as follows in the County of Hastings Directory of 1864-65:

Governor Gore and his wife, Lady Bella, travelled, it is said, through the Province and stayed a night at Meyers' Creek.

Shortly after, there met one evening at Mrs. Simpson's tavern the principal men of the village. Among those present were the two McNabbs. Feelings very loyal, and at the same time the importance of the village, it was suggested by one of them that the place should be named Belleville after the Lady Bella Gore. The happy suggestion received the hearty approval of all present and thereafter the village was so called.

The *Kingston Gazette* of August 24, 1816 chronicled the naming of the village, but the name was misspelled in the paper. It should have been "Bellville" instead of Belleville. The mistake was corrected in the September 7th issue of that year, when the spelling appeared as "Bellville." Just when it reverted to the present spelling of "Belleville" is not known.

KINGSTON, SEPTEMBER 7, 1816.

. . . .

ERROR CORRECTED.

We mentioned in our paper of the 24th ult. that the " New Town, formerly distinguished by the name of *Myers' Creek*, at the River Moira, was now called *Belleville*, &c." We were under the supposition, from the very pleasant situation of that town, that its name was derived from the French ; but we have since been informed, that it has been given the name of BELLVILLE, in honor of Lady Gore, " at the request and petition of a great number of the inhabitants of that town, and the township of Thurlow."

Notice in the *Kingston Gazette*, September 7, 1816.

From time to time the subject of how Belleville got its name is being discussed by historians. It has been suggested that Belleville might have been named after the early local merchant, Colonel William Bell who was also a teacher and an officer in the Hastings Militia and one of Captain Meyers' adversaries. There is also the theory that Belleville was named for its picturesque location on the Bay of Quinte and that the name was derived from the French for "lovely town".

Be that as it may. It seems more likely that the village was named in honour of Lady Bella Gore. Charming and beautiful as she was, she undoubtedly made a favourable impression on the male inhabitants of the village. And when on that warm August night at the tavern they had imbided freely of Mrs. Simpson's home-brewed beer and enjoyed a dance with Lady Bella, they composed a petition asking the Lieutenant-Governor to name the village after his wife.

Which husband would refuse such a request? A horseman was told to get ready, and before dawn he was on his way to Kingston carrying a notice to the *Kingston Gazette* announcing the birth of a new locality.

Lieutenant-Governor Francis Gore (1769-1853).

A Violent Election

by Gerald E. Boyce

Belleville has had its share of riots. The rebellion of 1837-38 witnessed the deaths of two local residents, the arrests of scores of suspected revolutionaries, and the wrecking of a Belleville newspaper office. The Grand Trunk Railway strike of 1876-77 saw the town's railroad engineers blockade the main Toronto-Montreal line for three days, until two hundred officers and men of the Queen's Own Rifles arrived from Toronto to restore law and order. And the elections of the nineteenth century frequently were accompanied by threats, intimidation, violence and general disorder.

Perhaps the most violent and exciting local election was that held in October, 1842, to elect a member for the Canadian Legislative Assembly (now known as the House of Commons). In the 1842 election, the government ordered two companies of soldiers from Kingston to Belleville to enable the election to proceed. Even then, only a small number of eligible voters were able to vote, and the whole election was finally declared invalid.

The story of the exciting 1842 election has been told for the first time in *Gentle Pioneers*, a book from the pen of Audrey Y. Morris.

In *Gentle Pioneers*, Audrey Morris tells the story of five related pioneers who came from the British Isles in the 1830's. The five were Susanna Strickland Moodie, noted writer and Belleville resident in the years from 1839 to 1869; J. W. Dunbar Moodie, Susanna's husband and the first sheriff of the Victoria District as Hastings County was known in the 1840's; Catherine Parr Traill, Susanna's sister and herself an important writer; Catherine's husband, Thomas Traill, and Samuel Strickland, the younger brother of Susanna and Catherine. All five settled in the Peterborough-Belleville area.

The election of 1842 finds its way into *Gentle Pioneers,* since this was one of the challenges faced by Dunbar Moodie. He served as returning officer in this contest between Tory Edmund Murney and Reformer Robert Baldwin.

Earlier, in 1841, Moodie had also served as returning officer when the same two candidates had contested the local election, but the earlier contest was somewhat tame by comparison.

In both contests, the Orangemen supported Murney of Belleville against Toronto Reform leader Baldwin who sought to bring the Hastings seat into the Reform fold.

Baldwin had won the first contest by thirty-six votes, whereupon Murney's supporters condemned both Baldwin and returning officer Moodie.

J. W. Dunbar Moodie, Sheriff of Hastings County, his wife Susanna Moodie (centre) and Miss Russell.

It was alleged that Moodie had refused to stop ruffians from bothering Murney's followers. Moodie was accused of favouritism. And, in fact, Moodie had entertained Baldwin in his home and had become a good friend of this cultured gentleman, so that the charges seemed to have some foundation. However, all records indicate that Moodie was an impartial returning officer and did a conscientious job in 1841.

When the polls opened at Belleville on October 3, 1842, the voting was interrupted by riots. Groups of armed citizens challenged each other and blocked the path of citizens who might vote for the opposing candidate.

Alarmed by this state of events, Moodie called up the militia and swore in special constables. Violence continued unchecked. Hence, Moodie asked for and received two companies of regular troops from Kingston.

Honourable Edmund Murney.

The troops arrived on Thursday, the fourth day in the six-day cycle of voting. Even their arrival failed to quell the disturbances, as Murney's supporters continued to block the routes leading to the poll.

Possible Baldwin voters, who would have to announce their preference publicly (as was the custom of the times) held back from the poll. Hesitating to use the troops against Murney's supporters and hoping to avoid further violence, Moodie waited.

However, since so few persons were able to vote (except for Murney's supporters), Moodie knew that he must do something. Therefore, he asked the government to allow the polls to remain open for more than the scheduled six-day period. Unfortunately, no extension was granted. Then on Friday, October 7, there were further attempts at riot, and Moodie closed the poll early. The poll was also closed early on Saturday for the same reason.

When the votes were tabulated, the count was four hundred and eighty-two for Murney and four hundred and thirty-three for Baldwin. But Moodie refused to certify that the election had been completed, since so few people had been able to vote. He called upon the Canadian Legislative Assembly to arrange a new election. This request was granted, and Murney and Baldwin again prepared to do battle.

Both sides were critical of Moodie for his handling of the 1842 election, and a different returning officer was appointed. He was William Hutton, first warden of the Victoria District (Hastings County). The new election saw Murney's victory confirmed.

The attack on Dunbar Moodie in connection with the two elections was only one part of a continuing campaign to remove the "intruder", as some people considered Moodie. There was resentment that an outsider from the Peterborough district should have been picked as the county's first sheriff.

MacKenzie's Left Wing Rebellion of 1837 was Comic Opera Act in Belleville

by Lenny Williamson

Belleville made the scene of the 1837 MacKenzie Rebellion with a comic opera act. The affair, staged as a farce involving incidents of mistaken identity, crossed signals, and general confusion, was enacted with a real talent for the inglorious.

Consider this cast of characters: an earnest church fund-raiser who was mistaken for a rebel agitator; a publisher whose printing plant was wrecked because a butter-fingered compositor made a typographical error; a blundering (and probably tipsy) officer who tripped over a bayonet in his front hall to become the war's only casualty; and a dedicated pacifist who donned cavalry uniform and instantly regretted it.

In 1837, William Lyon MacKenzie led a radical left-wing faction of the Liberal party in open revolt against the Family Compact in Upper Canada. The Tory favourites who sat in the Governor's Council and enjoyed the spoils of power had no love for the rabble crew that wanted to introduce that "American abomination", democracy, into British North America.

As MacKenzie made his demands for reform and those in power shouted him down with cries of "treason", feelings rose to fever pitch in Belleville.

The Governor called out the Hastings Militia and patriotic inhabitants rushed to Belleville to take their posts. Boisterous youths from remote farms tasted town life for the first time. At night, dandified in their British red coats, they loitered on street corners and imbibed too much at the numerous taverns.

Watchful mothers shooed their daughters into the house at nightfall and locked the doors. Careful shopkeepers barricaded their windows against military looters. The natives were restless and the stage was set for hysteria.

Against this background, John O'Carroll, grocery merchant on Front Street, devoutly launched his fund-raising appeal for the new St. Michael's Church. O'Carroll, as parish secretary, sat behind his shuttered windows each night, laboriously penning his requests for money to the Roman Catholics of the district. Each morning he stuffed the nearest mailbox with his campaign literature.

Soon the rumour spread that he was distributing rebel propaganda.

A crowd of soldiers gathered outside O'Carroll's store, smashed its way in, threw merchandise into the street and carried off a large part of the stock. The unfortunate O'Carroll was bundled off to Fort Henry for eight weeks and forced to sell his business at a loss.

In the crowd that gathered to watch the looters were two teen-aged boys, one of them an *Intelligencer* printer's apprentice, Mackenzie Bowell, who grew up to become Prime Minister of Canada. The other was A. T. Petrie, later an alderman. (In 1905 the two men combined to present testimony of O'Carroll's innocence to the Premier of Ontario. O'Carroll's two aged daughters received two hundred dollars each from an apologetic government.)

Another victim of the militia's mixture of patriotic and potable spirits was Samuel Hart, publisher of *The Plain Speaker*, a newspaper with reform sympathies. One day a printer made a common enough error — he replaced the royal coat of arms at the head of a proclamation with another engraving. His mistake was corrected before many copies were printed, but it was interpreted as a calculated insult.

The next evening *The Plain Speaker* printing shop was wrecked. The foreman, James Gardiner, recorded the event in his diary:

"The super-loyal (among them some of the Militia) attacked the printing office and threw much of the type into the street. The Loyalists engaged in this destruction stole a few things, among them a cloak and a pair of gloves of mine."

The cloak was supposed to have been carried to the then rear of the county.

Fear of an American take-over has been a perennial theme in Canadian history. During Rebellion years, militia officers slept with one ear cocked for the expected invasion alarm. One night, thanks to militiamen who got their signals crossed, it came.

SCENE OF REBELLION TRAGEDY
In this house, still standing on Bridge Street West, Captain James McNabb was
killed during the MacKenzie Rebellion .

Troops guarding prisoners in a tavern mistook a tolling fire-
bell as a signal that Reformers were attacking the tavern to free
the prisoners. They sounded a warning that the townspeople, in
their turn, mistook for the general invasion alarm.

Troops rushed to waken Capt. James McNabb, sleeping in his
new stone house half way up Bridge Street West hill. Roused by
the commotion in his front hall, the captain raced downstairs. In
the dim light he tripped and fell on the bayonet of a militiaman
who was running up to meet him. The captain died twenty-four
hours later of a deep abdominal wound. With black arm bands,
muffled drums and firing party, the Hastings Militia turned out to
bury Belleville's only Rebellion casualty with full military honours.

The military career of one Lieut. Farley of a hastily organized cavalry unit had a happier outcome. A member of a prominent
Quaker family and a dedicated pacifist, young Farley temporarily
forgot his principles when revolt threatened and ran off with his
horse to enlist.

By the time he was given his first military assignment, Farley was torn with conflict between his duties to God and to the state. He was ordered to carry a message to Cobourg directing troops of that area to Toronto to engage the rebels at Montgomery's Tavern. As a Quaker he could take no part in precipitating bloodshed. He solved his dilemma with pioneer ingenuity.

As soon as he had ridden out of sight of town, Farley dismounted, drew the nails from one horseshoe and led his mount by the bridle until he came to the first blacksmith's shop. There he explained that his horse had cast a shoe and waited patiently until the smith had replaced it. Once out of sight of the shop he repeated the performance. Leading his horse and stopping at every smithy along the way, Farley made it to Cobourg in a little over a week. His dispatch was received too late to make mustering of the troops feasible and Farley's conscience remained untroubled. As soon as he returned to Belleville he negotiated an honourable discharge.

With MacKenzie's flight to the United States the rebellion excitement gradually petered out. The militia was demobilized and the political prisoners released. Belleville forgot its role in the Rebellion, but the battle between Grit and Tory left a legacy of bitterness and deep scars.

Street Lights Not Necessary

Council meetings in 1857 were not much different from those of today. Back then as now, our City Fathers frequently could not agree among themselves on the merits of a proposed project.

Out of sheer curiosity, let's find out what it was they disagreed with in council on Wednesday evening, April 1st, 1857. That night the subject of street lights was on the agenda before Mayor Francis McAnnany and councillors: Hope, Kerr, Corby, Shanks, Wills, Brown, Clarke, O'Hare and Blacklock.

First, Mr. Shanks suggested that all lamp posts erected by the Gas Company should be painted. All were in favour, and the motion carried. However, when Mr. Shanks proposed, seconded by Wm. Kerr, that a special committee on Gas, Fire and Water be empowered to install a street lamp on Pinnacle Street in the vicinity of the Wesleyan Methodist Church, he encountered vigorous objections.

The old Pinnacle Street Methodist Church, built in 1831. Now site of new complex of Royal Canadian Legion, Branch 99.

Mr. Blacklock rose to his feet and said that he had actually no objection to the erection of a lamp post at the place recommended by Mr. Shanks, and it certainly would have been placed there long ago if not Messrs. Yeomans and Sawyer had strongly opposed it at the time the proposal had first been made. Another councillor, however, voiced his fear that if this location was lighted, the young men in town would be "standing in front of the church watching the pretty girls coming out".

Mr. Corby objected to the placing of a lamp post on this particular spot as being "utterly unnecessary". He pointed out that there was one lamp at the Market and another one at the corner of Pinnacle and Dundas Streets, and if the congregation wanted a street lamp in front of their church, they should place it there themselves.

Mr. O'Hare also objected giving as his reason that, if it was done for the Methodist Church, it would be proper to ask for a lamp post in front of the church to which he belonged. Lifting his finger and smiling, he added "as the objection formerly arose from fear that the young men would look at the pretty girls and you now wish to place a light there, the inference is, that the pretty girls have all left us."

After a lengthy debate the motion was lost. Yeas: Messrs. Shanks and Kerr. Nays: Dr. Hope, Messrs. Clarke, Corby, Wills, O'Hare, Brown and Blacklock.

The Town Council then adjourned.

The Almost-Visit of the Prince of Wales

by Nick and Helma Mika

Royal visits have always been great occasions in Belleville. These visits have become pleasant memories to a large segment of the local population.

Unfortunatly, not all such visits have been successful. In 1860, the Prince of Wales, oldest son of Queen Victoria, (later to become King Edward VII), came to Canada to officiate at the opening of Montreal's Victoria Bridge and to lay the cornerstone for the new Parliament Buildings at Ottawa. He also visited cities of Nova Scotia, New Brunswick and Upper and Lower Canada.

It was learned that His Royal Highness was going to visit Belleville on Thursday, the 6th of September. The Mayor, Dr. William Hope, issued a Proclamation, calling on the inhabitants of the town to observe that day as a holiday.

Belleville Town Council and Hastings County Council began the most lavish preparations for the occasion. A special committee of five drafted an address of the citizens' loyalty, but for some reason the town council rejected it after the mayor had already signed it. When town council presented their own congratulatory address, the mayor refused to sign. Each accused the other of non-co-operation. After a stormy meeting, council expressed its lack of confidence in the mayor and asked the reeve to sign the address.

The citizens of Belleville outdid every other place in the province with respect to beauty and grandeur of their decorations. The wharf, where the Prince was supposed to land, was beautifully adorned with evergreens and banners, and a roadway leading to a platform out in the street was constructed. Lined with an avenue of small balsams, the roadway was covered with scarlet cloth.

PRINCE of WALES
RECEPTION COMMITTEE.

NOTICE is hereby given, that the General Committee will meet each day at FOUR o'clock, in the Town Hall.

By order, R. L. INNES,
      Secretary.

August 16th, 1860.

COMMITTEE ON DECORATIONS.

NOTICE is hereby given, that the members of this Committee will meet at the Office of *INNES & MACLEOD*, at TEN o'clock, every day, Sunday excepted.

By order, R. L. INNES,
      Secretary.

August 16th, 1860.

Pleasure Trip to Quebec,
TO MEET THE
PRINCE OF WALES.

THE STEAMER

ST. HELEN,
Captain SMITH,

WILL leave Belleville for Quebec, on Monday, August 20th, at 10 o'clock, a.m., arriving at Quebec on Wednesday morning, where she will remain until Thursday evening, and then accompanying the Prince to Montreal, where she will remain for four days.

Fare for the Trip—$15,

This includes Board, State Rooms, or Berths, from the time the Boat leaves Belleville, until she returns.

Persons taking passage by this Boat, will be in Quebec in time to witness the arrival of the PRINCE, and his fleet, and his reception at Quebec, the Provincial Industrial Exhibition at Montreal, and the opening of the Victoria Bridge by the Prince, thus affording one of the most pleasant and interesting trips, yet offered to the public.

Within the town no less than nine great arches were erected, two of them by the Loyal Orange Lodge. Coming up Front Street, the first arch was built by Dr. Ridley. At the junction of Dundas and Front Streets, William Wallbridge erected another imposing arch. Just before reaching Bridge Street, the town constructed a very elaborate arch at public expense. On both sides of the arch, stretching across its entire length were the words "Welcome Albert Edward, Prince of Wales". The next two arches with the mottos "No Surrender" and "Faith" were erected by the Orangemen of Belleville, and these arches were the most massive and impressing ones in town. Along the main business streets flag-staffs of thirty to fifty feet in height were placed every few feet with Union Jacks, Royal Ensigns and streamers of red, white and blue flying from their tops. Every house in town was decked out with evergreens, banners, flags and ornaments. Crowns of flowers, handsomely formed, the Prince's Crests, and countless mottos and devices were to be seen everywhere in town.

All preparations for the Prince's welcome had been completed, when rumours began spreading through town and county that the Prince of Wales would not be visiting Belleville.

The Duke of Newcastle, Secretary of State for the Colonies, who was travelling with the Prince and was his adviser, had declared that His Royal Highness would not associate himself with any partisans and objected to "any ovation in which the religious or political display of any party is made public".

The Duke did not want to offend the Roman Catholics of Canada. He expressed his concern about the possibility of "religious feuds and breaches of the peace" if Orangemen were allowed to parade in full regalia in honour of His Royal Highness.

Steamer *Kingston*.

The steamer *Kingston*, carrying the Royal party, arrived in the city of Kingston at four o'clock Tuesday afternoon, but instead of landing, the boat anchored off shore.

The Duke of Newcastle sent word ashore that the Prince would not land at Kingston, unless the Orangemen put away their regalia, rolled up their colours and took down their arches. This the Orangemen refused to do.

The boat remained anchored in the stream until Wednesday afternoon, and then proceeded up the Bay.

When Bellevillians learned what had happened in Kingston, they hastily concealed all Orange emblems and flags, fearing that the same situation as in Kingston would develop here. Excitement ran high. The telegraph office was open till late and the wires were kept busy receiving and transmitting messages.

The *Kingston* with His Royal Highness and his party arrived at nine o'clock in the evening of September 5th, at the Belleville harbour. The approach of the steamer was announced by the firing of guns on the Court House hill and the ringing of the town's church bells. The boat anchored about a hundred yards from the wharf. The arrival took people by surprise as the Prince had not been expected until noon the following day.

That evening the mood in Belleville was jubilant. Bonfires were made, and bells rang. Windows were brightly lighted, and joyous people were milling in the streets. No Orange emblems or flags were to be seen.

Unfortunately, the next morning the steamer *Bay of Quinte* brought a number of demonstrators from Kingston. Their coming influenced Belleville Orangemen in their decision to carry out their original plans and take part in the celebrations, clad in their full regalia, with flags flying and bands playing.

When their intentions became known to the mayor, he summoned a deputation consisting of Messrs. Corby, Jellett and O'-Hare. They went on board the *Kingston* and were received by the Governor-General. The Belleville deputation explained the state of affairs and asked if an address would be received. His Excellency replied that this was not possible under the circumstances.

While the deputation was still on board, orders were given to the captain of the boat to get up steam. The Duke of Newcastle had decided that the Prince should not land in Belleville while the Orangemen displayed their colours.

The Hon. E. Murney then went on board hoping to conciliate matters and obtain from Sir Edmund Head a half-an-hour's time in which to convince the town's Orangemen to change their minds. However, before Mr. Murney had time to conclude negotiations, the boat was gone, steaming towards Cobourg.

According to the contemporary paper, a general feeling of indignation against the Governor-General "for leaving with such indecent haste, was manifest among the people.

"The Prince to whom they wished to do honour — for whom they had songs of welcome, and hearty, loyal British cheers — for whom they had decorated their houses and their streets — whom they were waiting to receive with all the gladness, all the heartiness, all the enthusiasm that could be conceived of, had anchored in their harbour, but was prevented from landing by his advisers."

Thousands of disappointed people remained at Belleville, including 1,500 town and county school children. As the paper tells it, "The children sang the National Anthem, and they sang it well, but their little hearts were sad because the youthful Prince was not there to hear them".

Jackson's Artillery Company from Kingston were also in Belleville, described as "a fine looking set of men, who fired a salute when the Prince left."

Disappointed though they were, Bellevillians tried to make the best of the situation. The procession of ladies and gentlemen on horseback came off under the superintendence of Geo. Taylor, Esq. There were about forty ladies and four hundred men and "they presented a fine appearance."

In the afternoon the leading Belleville Orangemen conferred to see what could be done about this humiliation. They decided to stage a procession up Front Street and then on to Pinnacle Street to the Dafoe House (Hotel Quinte) where they were addressed by the County Master, Thomas Wills, Esq. He stated that "all regretted, deeply regretted, that the Prince, through ill-advisers, did not land but that he was glad the Orangemen had maintained their rights."

He alluded to their attachment to their Sovereign, which no one could question, and hoped "they would part as they did on the 12th of July, in the honesty, integrity and purity of their motives." The crowd then gave three lusty cheers for the Queen and the Prince of Wales, and three groans for the Duke of Newcastle. The band from Kingston played "God Save The Queen".

In the evening there was a display of fireworks, and a great torch-light procession of the Order of the Physiogs. There were about one hundred horsemen and fifty men on foot, dressed in every conceivable style and form, and their performances were "certainly comical."

The town was crowded, and the reporter concludes "there was no accident, no fighting to mar the festivities of the day, except the picking of a few pockets and the gloom over all which marks the day as an important epoch in our history."

Moira River Floods

by Nick and Helma Mika

Every now and then the Moira River goes on a rampage in the spring, and Belleville faces the threat of a flood.

The first recorded flood in Belleville occurred in 1816. Surveyor Wilmott, who was engaged in laying out the town plot at the time, wrote in his diary on March 26: "This day the whole flat was overflown with water and was obliged to work upon the high ground".

The last major flood occurred in 1936. On March 12 of that year the Moira broke over its banks in the early morning hours. The *Intelligencer* described the scene:

> *At Cannifton . . . the ice broke away and in a roaring torrent unleashed its fury on the city. The area of lower Front Street from the four corners to the Bay of Quinte is impassable for pedestrians, while the area from Coleman Street to the foot of Murney's Hill, from the Bay of Quinte to West Moira Street is under water from three to seven feet and still rising.*

> *Residents used boats exclusively in Murney Ward and in some places it was possible to row a boat right through the door of the house. Children who had to come across the river to go to the collegiate had to be rowed from the foot of Murney Hill to the Lower Bridge.*

> *For hours during the early morning dogs howled in dismal protest of their fate, adding to the general confusion of strident voices, fire engine sirens, motor car horns and the swish of cars.*

Downtown business and traffic came to a standstill as pouring rains added to the misery of the spring flood. Front Street soon was a whirlpool of water and debris. Furniture was seen floating down the river and down streets. City and railroad engineers succeeded in blasting a channel from the open harbour to the mouth of the river a week later and the worst was over. Two hundred people were left homeless and losses ran into hundreds of thousands of dollars.

Front Street, 1936.

There were other serious floods of equally disastrous consequences. In 1868 the upper steel bridge over the Moira was carried away by an immense body of ice. Some areas were flooded to a depth of five feet, and the only means of escape was by boat. The *Daily Intelligencer* of March 17, 1868 reports:

If Sunday, the 15th of March, will be a memorable day in the history of Belleville, the 16th will deserve to stand by its side on the historic page. The great calamity which was as indelibly written on the face of the Moira as was the handwriting on the wall at Belshazzar's feast, came with terrible earnestness a short time before midnight last night. Nearly every one expected that when the jam above the Upper Bridge gave way it would take the Bridge with it and cause an immense amount of damage, but the appearance of the River at dark led to the belief that the ice would not move for some hours, and many were anticipating that after all the jam would gradually give way and the Bridge would be saved. But like many other pleasing anticipations it was not realized. The great shove took place about eleven o'clock last night, and those who saw by the dim gas-lights, the great field of ice moving down the stream, and the large cakes tossing and tumbling about amid the water and drift-wood like ghostly spectres, and heard the crashing, crackling noise of the falling timbers of a dozen buildings mingled with the fragments of the iron bridge, "mountainous in bulk, in one wild havoc crashed," will not soon forget it.

The immediate cause of the shove was the breaking up of the pond above Jas. Canniff's dam, and the destruction of a portion of the dam. It was an immense body of ice and logs, and gathering strength as it came down the rapid stream it piled upon the jam near the Upper Bridge, and sent it forward on its destined mission of destruction. The Iron Bridge gave way before it with scarcely a struggle, and was carried on the top of the field of ice below the Lower Bridge, portions of it lying in about the same place from which it was taken three years ago. The piers were swept to the bottom and the great mass increasing in bulk by the buildings which it brought with it moved majestically down the River. Fears were entertained for the safety of the Lower Bridge, and there was an immediate rush made for that. As the timbers and ice crashed against the piers and came up against the wood-work the bridge shivered and trembled like an aspen leaf, and it was expected every moment this would follow the fate of the Upper Bridge. But it nobly stood the shock, and the only damage it sustained was the breaking away of a few stones from the piers and a portion of the outside railing and foot-path being carried away. The wreck and ruin which followed the path of this great "shove" was terrible to witness, and it is impossible to form an estimate of the damage done.

There was severe flooding in the spring of 1885 causing heavy property damage and injuries to several people. A number of smaller houses were shifted from their foundations. Doors were burst open by the ice, windows smashed and furniture overturned, without a moment's warning. Mr. S. H. Phippen had five hundred cords of wood piled near his ashery. The whole lot, together with his carts, and wagons and a barn were carried off by the rushing waters.

South of Bridge Street, April 16, 1885.

The flood of 1886 went down in history as one of the worst the city experienced. The first ice jam formed near the harbour on January 10th and not until March 8th was the city free from flood water and ice. Streets, houses and stores had remained more or less flooded for fifty-seven days. At times as many as two hundred families were forced to leave their homes. The lower parts of the city known as the "Sawdust Flats" were suffering most. Shelters were set up on Pinnacle Street in the former Methodist Church.

On March 19, 1918 the *Daily Intelligencer* had this to tell:

> *With a rush and a rumble like a giant unleashed, the ice jam at the Upper Bridge broke well before dawn and the Moira River was at once turned into a rushing torrent.*

This was the beginning of a flood long to be remembered by those who witnessed and experienced it. By noon, on March 20, the ice had begun to shove down the river from the Upper Bridge, coming to rest against the footbridge. The dam it formed caused the Moira to overflow, and within a short time Front Street was under several feet of water. Most stable owners were forced to rescue their horses by boat, and the scene for a while was one of utter confusion.

In the afternoon the footbridge gave way and was carried down the river and piled into the Lower Bridge. The water broke through onto Coleman Street and ice blocks were carried as far as Everett Street, stranding residents in their homes.

On March 23rd the ice jam broke at the Lower Bridge and was swept towards the Railway bridge, where another jam formed. The water level rose once more, and as the Moira spilled over its banks, the water surged into Front Street, flooding stores and forcing firemen to vacate No. 1 Fire Hall at the corner of Dundas Street East.

Bellevillians since have learned to watch the Moira closely each spring, and modern methods of flood control help to prevent heavy losses. Hopefully, the floods of the past are a part of the city's history never to be repeated.

Bridge Street, West, 1918.

Damaged Foot Bridge, 1918.

James Street, looking north, 1918.

A Prominent Belleville Family

by Ruth Howard

If friends and city officials had realized the fame to follow the name of Corby, they might have kept more records of the young British immigrant who came to the lumbering village of Belleville about 1832 aboard a supply boat from Quebec. Henry Corby and his wife had just arrived in the New World, and Henry's qualifications of youth, ambition and a small knowledge of the baking trade learned as an apprentice in London hardly marked him as the great opportunist, or founder of a large industry. With only a sovereign in his pocket, so it has been said, he invested in merchandise, opened a tiny shop, and shortly after, started a bakery. By 1838, he had become the leading baker in the community. Then tragedy befell the Corby household when Henry's wife and three children were drowned in the Bay of Quinte after their sleigh broke through the ice near Massassaga Point. A few years later, Henry Corby bought the Point and made it a public resort as a memorial to his lost family.

Henry's second wife was a sister of the first Mrs. Corby, and the couple had twelve children, eleven of whom survived.

During the 1837 rebellion, Henry served as an unattached volunteer with a rifle company, then returned to Belleville where he contracted to supply troops encamped in the neighbourhood of Belleville. At the close of the rebellion he sold his bakery, and purchased the steamer *Queen* which he operated for four years between Kingston and Belleville, himself acting as captain. He became engaged in the buying and selling of grain, an enterprise which led to his operation of a grist mill, and ultimately of a distillery.

Long known as "Honest Henry Corby" for his fair dealing, integrity, and benevolence, it would seem that these factors were largely responsible for his success. Henry was filled with the spirit of freedom and the rights of man which made him speak up loud and clear at town meetings. His deep voice, logical thought and height of over six feet made him a leader, which indeed he was among the local Liberals. However, the Conservatives were in power, and Henry ran into strong opposition to his idea of putting a dam across the Moira for his grist mill, particularly in view of his plans for distilling whisky as a side-line. Whether it was a political put-down or serious objection to distilling whisky, the fact remains that his plans for a dam were stymied because he could not gain permission from authorities in Belleville. But Henry had friends beyond the town, and a group of them arranged for his mill site and dam four miles up the Moira. The community that arose around the site naturally became known as Corbyville after the mill opened in 1857, offering a grain cracking service to local farmers who also brought wagonloads of corn to be ground and sacked for cooking and for cattle.

The distillery started operating on a small scale two years later. Whisky was said to be almost a "staple item" among township farmers and those who brought their grain to the mill became the customers whose demands grew from a bottle to a demijohn.

Henry Corby's first mill and distillery.

The mill continued to operate for many years, but gradually became secondary to the growing distillery.

Where the original building and its two additions once stood is now the site of modern brick racks, distilling rooms, tanks and granaries.

Henry Corby continued to live in Belleville, driving daily to his plant in a phaeton drawn by a fine span of carriage horses. By the time the Liberals had gained power, shortly after the establishment of his mill, Henry Corby's popularity in Belleville and his leadership were confirmed. He was elected mayor for a two-year term; business activities prohibited his running for subsequent elections. But he returned to politics, this time as a member of provincial parliament, representing east Hastings as a legislator during the first year of Confederation.

Today, the Quality Control Centre has expert tasters who check each individual blend for flavour; but Henry Corby didn't need salaried staff for this work. The farmers who stopped with their wagonloads of grain were happy to oblige by sampling the whisky from the barrels. There were many horse and buggy trips to Corbyville from Belleville: to sample and to buy. In town and country, the fame of Corby's whisky grew — and indeed became a "spirited" part of local social life. At barn-raising or stumping bees, a dipper hung above a pail of whisky, which, needless to say, increased the tempo of the work amid the merriment. Through the townships, and then the provinces, the fame of "Corby's" grew.

Henry Corby, in addition to his business and political work was a member of the first board of police commissioners in Belleville, captain of the fire companies for several years, and a long time president of St. George's Society. He was generous to humanitarian services, and the large flower and vegetable gardens around his home were almost public property where those of lesser means were free to help themselves.

Henry Corby died in October 1881, and his second son, also named Henry, took over the distillery which grew rapidly under his direction. More aggressive and modern-minded in merchandising policies than his father, the second Henry Corby built a suite of offices and a warehouse at the corner of Front and Market Streets, a building presently occupied by several offices. He quickly saw the advantages of bottling whisky for resale rather than selling it by the barrel or to those who brought their own containers. The aged whisky in barrels was brought to the Belleville warehouse for bottling until a bottling operation was installed at Corbyville, along with spurs from the two railways running up to the plant from Belleville.

Young Henry also imported wines and Scotch whisky, and engaged in the tobacco business. By the time he retired he had built up an estate worth well over a million dollars. His philanthropies were even greater than those of his father. He purchased

Senator Henry Corby.

the Merchants Bank building on Pinnacle Street, and refitted it into the Corby Public Library; contributed constantly to St. Thomas' Anglican Church; gave strong financial backing to the Belleville hospital; provided the city with Corby Park, now noted for its beautiful rose gardens.

Henry Corby married Maria Courtney in 1872, and the couple had three daughters.

As the city population grew, Henry Corby was a sponsor and instigator in almost every forward step: social, cultural, or industrial. And a political change had taken place in the Corby family: they had become as strongly Conservative as they had once been Liberal. Like his father, young Henry served in parliament — (but in the opposite camp) from 1888 to 1900. As a fitting climax to his career as a statesman and a public benefactor, the Canadian government named him a senator. Great honour and prestige accompany the title of Senator, bestowed upon only a few in each generation.

The bridge across the Bay of Quinte was first called Corby Bridge, promoted by the civic-minded gentleman who also promoted the Quinte Hotel. He was a charter member of several clubs which have resolved themselves into the present Belleville Club; built a set of public baths and a pavilion in Victoria Park, and improved the Massassaga Park.

*   *   *

When a young tobacco house salesman, Mortimer Davis called on the Senator in 1905, Henry mentioned his willingness to sell out and his desire to retire and travel; he had made his fortune. Davis raised the money to buy the business, became president of the company, and was subsequently knighted Sir Mortimer Davis because of his important industrial contributions to the British Empire.

The distillery burned down in 1907 and was rebuilt. In 1914 it suspended operations for the duration of World War I, but during World War II it converted entirely to industrial alcohol production for war time use.

Senator Corby died during a trip to Honolulu in 1918, eleven years after selling out the distillery for an estimated million dollars. In the same year the H. Corby Distillery Company Limited was sold out to Canadian Industrial Alcohol Limited, a holding company which later acquired Robert McNish and Company, Glasgow, Scotland. The J. M. Douglas Company and Wiser's Distillery Limited were also purchased outrightly.

In 1950, it was decided to give the Corby name first prominence and the parent company became H. Corby Distillery Limited.

Belleville General Hospital

Belleville Hospital, 1886.

In 1879 there was not a single hospital existing between Toronto and Kingston. A group of public-spirited women in Belleville saw the grave need for an organized society to look after the poor, sick and friendless of the community who had no one to care for them.

It all began when Mrs. Harriet Jacques, wife of the Principal of Albert College, appealed to the women in the city to unite and form such an organization. On November 18, 1879, the Women's Christian Association came into being as a result of her efforts. The first officers elected at the inaugural meeting were: Mrs. J. R. Jacques, President; Mrs. N. Jones, Mrs. Wm. Ponton, Miss Bilbrough, Vice-Presidents; Miss G. G. Osbourne, Recording Secretary; Mrs. J. H. Holden, Corresponding Treasurer.

The next step was to draw up a constitution. After much discussion, thought and suggestions, aims and objectives were boiled down to a practical form. Eighty members obtained a charter, registered at Toronto on June 2, 1880, which gave them the power to build a hospital and a home for the needy.

The Happy Worker's Room.

One would have thought Bellevillians on the whole, even if they were not wildly enthusiastic about the idea, would have at least accepted it in a kindly and tolerant state of mind. Not so. Attacked by newspaper, city council and people on the street, the women of the Association were accused of attracting the poor of the county to be supported by the city.

While the building of a hospital was the great aim, the newly-formed "W.C.A." was willing to start in a small way, for they knew that the immediate and urgent need was a home for the destitute. However, landlords were loath to rent a house for this purpose, fearing it might depreciate the value of their property. A place was finally secured on the west side of the river, opposite the International Hardware Company. Furniture, bedding and dishes were solicited in a door-to-door drive.

Once the home was established, the city granted three hundred dollars a year towards its upkeep. In the meantime, funds were being raised for a hospital. For five years the women laboured, talked, sold home-made things and held rummage sales.

But funds were not the only thing the women had to worry about. There was the matter of a lot for the hospital. In 1816, when the village was first surveyed, a large lot at the corner of Victoria Avenue and Church Street had been set aside for a hospital. It was later declared unsuitable for this purpose. The

Association proposed another site along the bay shore, but ran into violent opposition to their plans. Some people seemed to think that the city was being robbed of its property. Nevertheless, the old lot was sold to St. Michael's Church, and on July 25, 1885, Mrs. Jones turned the first sod at the present site of the hospital. On July 20, 1886, the combined hospital and home for the aged was formally opened. Mrs. Jacques did not see her dream come true. She had died in April of 1880.

The growing population of the city and the county soon required more care, and so in 1890 the east wing was built and used for elderly patients.

Female Public Ward.

In 1909, because the buildings were again over-crowded, the ladies of the Women's Christian Association decided on a further building program, adding the south wing, which was completed in 1911.

The Board of Governors was reorganized in 1922 and gentlemen came into the picture for the first time. The Board was made up of nine ladies, two gentlemen, chosen by the Women's Christian Association, two appointed by the City Council, one by County Council, and two members of the Medical Staff.

Fun from the Directory

SOME AMUSING GROUPINGS OF THE NAMES OF OUR CITIZENS

The County of Hastings Directory for 1889, is intended as a book of reference rather than a source of amusement, but from that portion of it which gives the names of the residents of the city we give the following interesting resume, which we trust will be found instructive as well as amusing:

The Smiths are, of course, the most numerous, there being 27, and what is somewhat remarkable, they are all genuine Smiths — no Smyths, or Smythes amongst them. Next come the Thompsons, 23, next Clarkes, 21, then Robertson or Robinson, 17, Brown 20, Taylor 15, Johnson or Johnston 14, Reid, Reed, or Read 15, Wilson 12, Young 12, Cook 11, Lazier 11, McCoy 10.

1889.

DIRECTORY

—OF THE—

COUNTY OF HASTINGS,

—CONTAINING—

A FULL AND COMPLETE LIST OF HOUSEHOLDERS OF THE CITY OF BELLEVILLE, OF EACH TOWN, TOWNSHIP AND VILLAGE IN THE COUNTY, AND OF THE TOWNSHIP OF AMELIASBURGH, PRINCE EDWARD COUNTY, A CLASSIFIED LIST OF TRADES AND PROFESSIONS OF BELLEVILLE, TOGETHER WITH OTHER INFORMATION, LOCAL AND PROVINCIAL, AND ADVERTISEMENTS OF THE PRINCIPAL BUSINESS HOUSES, EMBELLISHED WITH

LITHOGRAPHIC MAPS

OF THE COUNTY, BELLEVILLE, AND THE PRINCIPAL VILLAGES.

BELLEVILLE:
PUBLISHED BY THE INTELLIGENCER PRINTING AND PUBLISHING CO.

1889.

The trades are represented by 4 Bakers, 1 Brasier, 3 Butlers, 1 Carman, 1 Carrier, 2 Carters, 21 Clarkes, 2 Chandlers, 5 Colemen, 11 Cooks, 4 Coopers, 1 Docter, 2 Dunns, 1 Falconer, 1 Foster, 4 Fullers, 4 Gardeners, 2 Goldsmiths, 1 Harper, 5 Hunters, 2 Marshalls, 1 Mason, 4 Millers, 3 Miners, 2 Naylors, 1 Nurse, 3 Pages, 3 Potters, 1 Pyman, 1 Sawyer, 2 Slaters, 27 Smiths, 15 Taylors, 2 Turners, 1 Thrasher, 2 Yeomans, 2 Stewards.

Of the animal kingdom we have of birds and beasts, 4 Bulls, 2 Coons, 1 Coney, 1 Drake, 2 Foxes, 2 Harts, 1 Herron, 2 Hoggs, 3 Martins, 1 Nightingale, 1 Teal, 2 Woodcock, 1 Wolfe, 1 Roe, 1 Starling, 3 Lyons, and as might be expected where we possess 3 Watters and 4 Lakes we have of fish — 2 Fish — variety unamed, 3 Herrings, 2 Soles, 1 Ling, 1 Sturgeon, 1 Spratt, and what is more remarkable in fresh waters, 1 Whale, the latter is to be seen at Albert College.

Our variety of vegetables is few, for while we have 2 Seeds, 3 Roots, 2 Husks and 2 Cobbs, we only have 1 Bean and 1 Pepper, and of fruits we only possess 1 Berry, 3 Newberrys, 2 Lemons and 1 Cherry. Not much attention is given to horticulture, for we have only 1 Flower and 1 Rose. Notwithstanding we have not a church, we have a number of church dignities, there being no less than 3 Popes, 1 Bishop, and for him 1 Crozier, 2 Abbotts, 2 Parsons, 3 Deacons, 1 Elder. Our Aristocracy consists of 1 Marquis, 6 Earls and 1 Knight. The only jewels we possess are five Diamonds. That our citizens are modest in dress is found in the fact that the only colours we have are Brown, Green, Black, Grey and White. Two are ever at your Serviss. Where there are 3 Potters one would expect to find 2 Potts. If any one should get into a Peck of trouble or into any Pickle, we have one Ransome to offer, and he is not a Petty one. For one Maiden and 3 Dames we have one Mann, but several Fellowes. All the year round we have May and several Maybees. We also have Hay and Grass. Our Diet comes Daly, and although it is a Crumb it is a Grant, that is Good. They are honest people, albeit one is Robb, 2 Steele, and another is a Skinner. Our only weapons of defence are 1 Cannon, 1 Gunn, and 1 Lance. In a population of 10,000 one Row is not much. One of our citizens is ever Ready, another Tardy, while 3 are Spry, 2 are Stout, 1 Short and 1 Long. One is Sweet and 2 are Pretty; 3 are Strong and 1 Tremble's; 3 are Good, several Love, and 2 Haight. One has Grace, another Mercy. One is Sharp, and 2 Tickell. One is Large and 3 are Biggar. Proving that ghosts exist we have one real Bogle; we have Frost all the year round. Hope and Mercy live not far apart. We have 9 Mills, but only 4 Millers. For our one House we have one Tennant, and it possesses 1 Garratt, 2 Halls, 3 Keys and 8 Bells. Five persons only are always Wright, and 1 is Worth something; 12 will ne'er be old, as they are ever Young. What is the use of providing a drill shed when the only military officers we have are 2 Sergeants? In addition to the Mock Parliament we have 1 real Parliament, and for this Parliament but one Mann. Whether the City Council provides electric lights or not, we always have 5 Moons. An extra-ordinary thing is that while we have no sun or showers a Rainbow can always be seen, and yet we have no night, but continual Day. In our 2 Walls there is but one Wickett, and on our one Bush one Wragg. One family has Souls. In one Volume are three Pages. The manager of the Telephone Co. is appropriately named Stringer. For bad school boys there are 3 Kanes, and for good ones 1 Holiday. In the area of our city the landscape is varied, as we have 2 Watters, 4 Lakes, 2 Marshs, 1 Cataract, 1 Forrest, 3 Woods, 1 Redwood and 1 Greenwood; 3 Hunters are all the sports we have. Only one inhabitant is a Riddell. That one of the ills that flesh is heir to affects us is proven by having 4 Boyles, but to rest in we have 2 Bowers, 2 Booths, with one Couch. "One Price only" is our one Merchant's motto. For the most disconsolate we have a Crumb of comfort. Two citizens prefer to be Creepers, while 7 are Walkers and one would rather Wade. One can Doo, while two can Doolittle. The places represented are Kingston, London, Mayo, Troy, Hudson, Kent, Lyons, Shannon, Severn. We have very little foreign population, for 1 English, 4 Welch, 1 French and 1 Pole represents it all. Because we have but one Freeman, it does not follow that all the rest are slaves. Although there are 3 Downs, there are no ups, and yet there are 4 Hills, but no dales. The most popular christian name is William, next John, then James, then George, next Thomas and Henry. Amongst unusual christian names are Friend, Sebastian, Shadarack, Adolphus, Elgar, Willis, Courtland, Dominick, Mose, Delos, Roman, German, Prosper, Merconess, Milton, Byron, Newlove, Casper, Emanuel, Nixon, Nathan, Merrick, Alonso, Petro, Clavrie, Haldrake, Norman, Raymond, Constantine and Alphonso.

*   *   *

The 1966 Directory reflected fascinating changes, for instance the 1889 edition cost two dollars; the 1966 edition cost fifty dollars. Belleville had a population of 11,500 in 1889 and required twenty-one aldermen to administer civic business; in 1966 only ten men were needed to do the job. Population 32,000.

Nineteen doctors served 11,500 people in 1889; forty-two look after three times that number in 1966. Only twenty-two societies functioned in 1889 including the Mechanics Institute and Library Association. Charitable, fraternal and social institutions take over a page in the 1966 edition. Now one hundred and six firms are devoted to keeping the family jalopy on the road, compared to the nine carriage and wagon manufacturers supplying means of transportation in 1899. The city has nineteen hotels and motels now, compared with twenty-one in 1889. The old directory lists six restaurants and three ice cream parlors. The 1966 directory lists forty-one.

Most drastic changes reflected in the pages of the directories are the number of lawyers in the community. Legal firms totalled thirty-three in 1889; 1966 with triple the population, only twenty-three are listed.

Perhaps coincidence alone is the reason for the advice, printed on a page of aphorisms at the back of the old directory; "Don't go to law unless you have nothing to lose; lawyer's houses are built on fool's heads."

MADAME MONSUER,
SEEING MEDIUM,
Astrologist and Phrenologist,

HAS arrived in Town, and will remain a short time at the

ANGLO–AMERICAN HOTEL.

☞Please Walk Up-Stairs.☜

Reception Room first door to right. Private
Room No. 6, second flat,

Where she can be consulted in regard to future events, relative to sickness, health, distant friends, place of residence in future, and even the complexion and condition in life of the future husband and wife, and will answer any question given her on any subject whatever, agreeable to the person propounding the same. By what means she can do this last is not known to herself, and barely knows as others know—she can do it.

She is descended from a long line of French Astrologists, and can also tell the future by the hand and cards.

The Grand Trunk Railway Strike in Belleville

by Nick and Helma Mika

October 27, 1856, the day the first train passed through Belleville, was a gala occasion for the town's inhabitants. Crowds lined the tracks to see the ten passenger cars and two wood-burning engines steam into Belleville station on the train's initial Montreal-Toronto run.

The train was filled to capacity with celebrities and officials of the Grand Trunk Railway, operators of the new line.

When the train pulled into Belleville the passengers were officially greeted by Mayor John O'Hare and members of his council.

Express train.

Belleville Grand Trunk Station.

The coming of the railway was a valuable asset to the economy and progress of both the town and the county. The town's economy back then was based on lumbering, agricultural products, and diversified manufactured goods. Belleville was a very prosperous town, but there were signs of labour unrest.

Section gangs on the Grand Trunk were not happy with their pay and had threatened to obstruct the train on its initial run. The train ran at a slow pace in case trouble might occur, but the workmen did not carry out their threat.

Belleville soon became an important railway centre. In 1867 the first locomotive shop was built here, and later a second shop was added to accommodate twenty-four engines. The Belleville shops employed one hundred and twenty people.

In the 1870's the Grand Trunk Railway announced plans of further expansion in Belleville. However, there were signs of a slow-down in the economy on the horizon, and as was to be expected, these plans had to be shelved temporarily. In December, 1876, the company decided to cut train services, and two days before Christmas, sixty-six of three hundred and fifty-seven engineers on the Grand Trunk System were dismissed.

It was a cold winter. The men faced a bleak holiday without the benefit of unemployment insurance. To make matters worse the company had laid off some of its long-time employees and retained others at a lower pay. The company also had dismissed several employees who had joined the newly formed "Brotherhood of Locomotive Engineers of North America".

Predictably, the workers were angry, but in an effort to avoid a strike, they presented their grievances to the company's General Manager, J. Hickson, in Montreal:

Montreal, Dec. 29, 1876.
Jos. Hickson, Esq., General Manager, G.T.R.
Dear Sir,—We the undersigned, a committee appointed to represent the Locomotive Engineers in your employ, do hereby notify you that unless the following propositions are acceded to the engineers in your employ will stop work on Friday, the 29th inst., at 9 p.m.

(1) That all firemen promoted to engineers shall receive for the first year the second class rates of wages paid on the division they are employed upon. After that they shall receive full rates, or that known as first-class rates.

(2) All engineers employed shunting shall receive $2 per day, and, if transferred to the road at the expiration of one year, shall receive first-class rates.

(3) No engineer or firemen to be discharged for any cause without a fair and impartial trial, and his guilt established beyond a doubt.

(Signed,) J. Eaton, J. Cardell, E. Taylor, J. O'Brien, C. Pickring, J. Ferguson, J. Fitzpatrick, A. McNaughton, T. Hollinrake, T. Rennick.

The Grand Trunk refused to comply with the workers' demands. Under the law, no engineer was allowed to leave his engine without facing severe punishment. However, as a precaution, Mr. Hickson hired non-union men, who were willing to work, and sent them to Belleville.

This was the signal to strike.

The company realizing that a strike was imminent, kept most of its trains in terminals. However, five trains, still on the line, were brought to a standstill. Some of them could not reach their destination in time, some were stranded miles from stations.

According to the contemporary account in the local paper, "On Saturday afternoon (December 30, 1876) the strikers succeeded, either by intimidation or persuasion, in inducing the men, who had been sent to keep the line open, to become accomplices by joining the Brotherhood." In order to prevent the passage of a train, the strikers blocked the main line by derailing two snowploughs.

The Grand Trunk at once requisitioned the Mayor, W. A. Foster, for assistance, and the men of No. 1 Company of the 49th Rifle Regiment were ordered to turn out. It was nearly midnight before thirty men could be assembled. Under the command of Capt. Harrison, they were conveyed in sleighs to the station to guard the railway company's property.

The Road Master, Mr. Marshall, was kept busy the rest of the night erecting the derailed snowploughs, but while workmen were clearing the tracks at the eastern end of the yard, the strikers would throw one of the ploughs off the tracks at the western end.

The Montreal Express was expected to come through Belleville about ten p.m. and trouble was anticipated. However, the engineer of this train, being afraid of violence because of threats made at Napanee by the strikers there, would not come any further than Shannonville, where the train remained for ten hours.

There were a considerable number of passengers on the train, and many were waiting to proceed westward. On Sunday morning, Mr. Davis, the Mechanical Superintendent, requested the "Rifles" to assist him in the removal of a locomotive from the sheds to be sent to Shannonville to pick up the train. A shot was fired at the engine on her way to Shannonville, but no one was hurt. When the train finally arrived in Belleville, the strikers congregated on and about the platform, determined to prevent the departure of the train, in spite of the military.

At last an engineer was found in the person of Mr. Hartins, one of the men the company had brought here some days before. He was willing to take the train through to Toronto.

A locomotive was taken from the shed and backed slowly down to the cars to be coupled. It was then that violence erupted.

The strikers rushed towards the engine, hurling stones and some brandishing revolvers. Commanding Officer Harrison gave the order to "fix bayonets" and the militiamen surrounded the engine. The strikers, however, succeeded to place an iron bolt into the slide-bar and partly paralized the locomotive, so that it had to be taken back to the shed.

The engineer was chased by the crowd. Somebody fired a shot. This infuriated the rioters, they threatened to kill him, and the mob resorted to violent acts of vandalism. They captured the en-

PROCLAMATION.

A T a Meeting of a number of the Magistrates of the Town of Belleville and County of Hastings, held this second day of January, 1877, it was moved by the Hon. B. Flint, and seconded by A. L. Smith, Esq ,

" That the Mayor of the Town of Belleville be requested to issue a Proclamation warning all persons not having lawful business to transact at the Grand Trunk Railway Station in the Town of Belleville or within its vicinity, not to assemble, loiter, or remain in or about said premises, during the continuance of the disturbance now existing at and about said Station, under the penalties of 31st Vic. cap. 70."

In compliance with the above request and by virtue of the power vested in me as Mayor and Chief Magistrate of the Town of Belleville, I hereby issue this my Proclamation warning and forbidding all persons, not having lawful business at the Grand Trunk Railway Station of the Town of Belleville, not to assemble, loiter or remain in or about the premises of the Grand Trunk Railway Station during the continuance of the difficulties referred to in the above resolution.

Any disobedience of this Proclamation subjects the offender or offenders to the penalties of the above recited act, viz.: To be "guilty " of felony and shall be liable to imprison- " ment in the Provincial Penitentiary for life " or for any other term not less than two " years, or to be imprisoned in any other jail " or place of confinement for any term less " than two years."

W. A. FOSTER.
Mayor.

Belleville, Jan. 2, 1877.

gineer and severely beat him, despite the gallant efforts of Colonel Brown to protect him. Hartins was taken in a sleigh downtown where he received medical attention.

At that point the company decided not to move the express train to Toronto. Captain Harris assembled his volunteers and took them back to the armories. Later he was criticized for not taking a more positive stand against the strikers and not assisting vigorously enough when help was needed.

Mayor Foster, determined to maintain order, issued the following proclamation which was posted in town and at the railway station:

In the meantime, one hundred men of the 15th Battalion Argyll Light Infantry under Lt.-Col. S. S. Lazier had been ordered out in the morning. By two p.m. only thirty men had been collected. Many of the men were sympathizing with the strikers, and others refused to turn out because of "bad treatment" they had received from the government.

At four o'clock in the afternoon, commanded by Captain Crozier, the men proceeded to the station where they were placed on guard at the two engine sheds. During the night another attempt was made to start the train but all efforts failed. Consequently, it was resolved to wait until a larger force of military could be assembled. The soldiers of the 15th Battalion were ordered back to the armories.

County Attorney, C. L. Coleman, was informed by the Government that the rioters must be subdued and the road opened to traffic, and if the local military force was not sufficient, he was told to procure additional troops from Toronto or Kingston. Immediately following this development, Mayor Foster sent a telegram to Militia Headquarters in Toronto. The telegram was received by Lieutenant-Colonel W. S. Durie late in the afternoon of New Year's Day. The same night one hundred and seventy men of the Queen's Own Rifles were assembled under the command of Lieutenant-Colonel Otter. At 7:30 a.m. the next day, they left for Belleville on a special train consisting of two engines and eighteen passenger cars.

In Belleville the morning passed uneventful. The Mayor's proclamation requesting all persons who had no legitimate business at the Grand Trunk Station to refrain from going there, was simply ignored, and large numbers of citizens proceeded to the station.

The train from Toronto conveying the "Queen's Own" arrived at Sidney Station, six miles west of Belleville, about nine o'clock. Men with fixed bayonets were on each locomotive. The Mayor of Belleville and Mr. John Bell, Solicitor for the railway company, drove out to Sidney Station to confer with Col. Durie as to their future conduct. Mr. Bell drove back to town and the Mayor remained on the train.

Rumors were flying that overhead bridges had been taken over by the mob and obstructions had been placed on the iron bridge over the Moira River. Mr. Marshall, the Road Master, went to investigate but found nothing wrong. The train was then ordered into the station and approached Belleville at 11:30. There were five companies on the train and each man had twenty rounds of ball cartridges and orders to use his bayonet if necessary.

The train was met at the west end of the station by a large crowd of men, women and children. There was a good deal of hooting, yelling, and throwing of stones and sticks at the engines, but the station was reached safely, and crowds gathering around the engines were kept back.

Two hours later the Montreal express train was watered and coaled, and signal was given to proceed to Toronto. Soldiers walked along the side of the train as it moved out of the station. A number of boys and strikers got on the cars and tried uncoupling and separating the train, but the men in charge — twenty-five of the Queen's Own — were able to beat them off.

The train was the first to leave Belleville station since Friday night, when the strike had started. Fifteen minutes later, orders were given to prepare an eastbound train. Strikers again attempted to stop the train. Violence erupted and it was necessary to move the entire contingent of soldiers to push back the mob. However, they managed to throw the engine off the track by displacing a switch and workmen had great difficulties to get it back on the rails. During the repair a volley of stones was hurled and several pistol shots were fired from the crowd.

One of the strikers who refused to move from the engine received a severe wound from a bayonet and was carried to the Lodge Room of the Brotherhood where surgeon Thorburn dressed the wound. Several others were also injured by bayonets.

Realizing that the troops meant business, the mob fell back and the locomotive got safely under way to Montreal.

After the train had left, Mr. Davis received a telegram from headquarters stating that a settlement was about to be reached between the company and the men on strike. Five minutes later another message came, this time from John Eaton, chief of the Toronto Grand Trunk division, saying "All is settled".

The settlement of the strike was a clear victory for the workers. They were well satisfied even though not all their demands had been met.

Militia on the Market Square.

From Mill to Station Street

by Ruth Howard

Station Street today may be one of the less attractive streets in Belleville, but it is still a busy commercial area, a factor which has marked this area since its beginnings in the late eighteenth century. It ranks with Dundas, Bridge, Victoria and Front Streets in historic value, and was one of the original streets when Belleville was a small village, settled mostly by United Empire Loyalists. In fact, Mill Street as it was originally named was a well-known street when the area now known as Front Street was still a red cedar swamp.

Mill Street was a natural name for the rough, boggy old road where several sawmills were located during the late eighteenth and nineteenth centuries. The town of Thurlow, or Meyers' Creek as Belleville was then called, was the destination for the thousands of logs sent down river from points north where there were several logging camps. The Moira River was much deeper and more rapid than it is today. The River was called Sagonaska by the Indians, and renamed Singleton's Creek by the first white settlers. When Captain John Walden Meyers constructed a dam and built a sawmill in 1790, the river and settlement became known as Meyers' Creek. The village began to form a little distance below the Captain's mill, which is a significant factor in the history of Mill Street. The Belleville Directory of 1879-80 states:

. . . Captain John W. Meyers, having purchased from Mr. Taylor the north half (more or less) of his lot for $100, in 1790, erected a dam on the site of what is now known as Bleecker's or Meyers' dam, where he built a mill, the only one between Port Hope and Napanee, and in 1794 constructed the famous old brick house which, until 1876, stood on the northern brow of the hill, and was the oldest brick house in Upper Canada.

As a convenience for ascending and descending between the Meyers' house and mills, the Captain had built a set of steps into the side of the hill, leading down onto what is now Great St. James, another old industrial area where railway tracks run right along the street.

Captain John Meyers, being a farsighted and industrious businessman, added a gristmill to his enterprises. Farmers came long distances to have their grinding done. Some even came on foot, each toting a bag of grain on his back. A part of Meyers' Mill still exists on the premises of A. Safe & Son, and going down to the river, one will even find a trace of the first mill dam. The erection of Meyers' Mill has been credited with attracting many new settlers to the village. Meyers further expanded his enterprises by operating a trading post and setting up a distillery. Unfortunately, the Meyers' house was torn down in 1876, and an historic landmark vanished. But the name of Captain John Meyers remains linked with Belleville's history. There are many stories about him as a soldier, as a true Loyalist and an entrepreneur which are almost legendary. He died in 1821. Some of his descendants still live in the Quinte district.

View on Moira River from Station Street.

The name of Meyers' Creek was changed to Belleville in 1816, and was originally spelled without the "e". The settlement then became a place on the map. A mill road leading from Meyers' mills to the landing place at the Bay became the guide line for Front Street. Belleville was set up as an independent municipality in 1836, incorporated as a town in 1850, and from that year onwards made more rapid progress. It was incorporated as a city on December 31, 1877. The event was celebrated on July 1, 1878.

In the first half of the ninetenth century, Belleville was mainly noted for its lumbering business, and apparently was still humming with this activity past the middle of the century, according to this little rhyme taken from *Mosaic of Belleville*

I remember dear old Belleville way back in '59,
When lumbering was the leading trade, and business was fine.
Our harbour with shipping was crowded, the saws' hum filled
*   the air,*
When whisky was 12 cents a quart and sold most everywhere.

When the pine limits became somewhat exhausted, the lumber business began to drop off, but other branches of industry sprang up to replace it. The largest share of the new industry was located on Mill Street.

Mill Street was to become the scene of further progress. Railways were being built, and after some controversy as to whether the station would be built in Belleville or Cannifton, the former won this coveted aid to industry. On October 27, 1856, most of the local populace came to see the first through train from Montreal to Toronto when it arrived at the new Grand Trunk Station on Mill Street.

The Grand Trunk established one of its shops near the Belleville station, and our city has ever since been a railroad centre. The first station house was a rather small stone structure which still exists if one wishes to take note of this in the midst of the buildings added since that time.

Under the heading of "Manufacturers", the Belleville Directory of 1879-80 states:

There are now in Belleville three foundries which do an extensive trade; 1 axe factory, the best in Canada, and one of the most extensive; 5 sash factories; 3 gristmills; 2 furniture manufactories; 1 broom factory; 4 sawmills; 2 cigar factories;

4 carriage manufactories; 1 pottery; 1 manufactory of carriage bodies and bent stuff for carriages; 1 sewing machine factory, whilst just without the borders of the city are two large brick manufactories, and also six sawmills.

In looking through the advertisements in the old Directories, is is interesting to note that the largest share of these industries were found on Mill Street. Some of the ads do not give the street location; perhaps they felt it unnecessary, due to their fame in such a small town.

Lott's Woollen Mill was established in 1876, and was located at the site of Captain Meyers' mill, utilizing the dam and the old buildings. It handled up to forty thousand pounds of wool a year, and made tweeds, flannels, stocking yarn and other woollen materials. In 1885 the first pole lines were erected, and electricity, the new boon to industry was generated at Lott's Woollen Mill.

The traveller, in order to reach the dock or other parts of town, and the traveller by boat who wished to reach the railway station, was certain to go along Mill Street where he should be impressed with the industrial progress of Belleville. Mill Street extended from the Upper Bridge to the Grand Trunk Railway station, and was where, as noted in the Directories, "are situated some of our largest foundries and factories."

Under *Foundries and Agricultural Works*, the Directory of 1869-70 states:

The Messrs. Brown are the largest manufacturers in the town. Their premises front on Mill, Foundry and Church Streets, and cover a large extent of ground. During the past year, a large portion of their premises have been rebuilt. and now they have one of the finest and most complete establishments in the Province of Ontario.

From this historic sketch of the past, we can note the vast contribution of Mill Street to Belleville's growth. But as the railway station gained more importance than the dwindling mill business over the years, it is not surprising that somewhere along the way, the street was renamed Station Street.

Hugh McKinnon: the Strongest Strong Arm of the Law

by Harry Mulhall

". . . A row occurred in Buchanan's Hotel last night among a party of young men who were drinking. The row becoming general, resulted in the breaking of a number of bottles by the crowd, who seemed masters of the situation when the Chief of Police arrived on the scene and summarily landed the whole crowd in the street."

No need for the *Intelligencer* of the day to name the chief of police who performed that single-handed feat of law enforcement one summer's night in 1878. Everyone in the Quinte district knew The Chief, and every community in the province might well have envied Belleville for having such a man as its chief constable.

For in Hugh McKinnon the community of Belleville — then Canada's youngest city — had literally and figuratively one of the strongest arms of the law anywhere in North America. And if ever an Ontario town needed such a man to embody the law at the time, that Ontario town was Belleville.

When he strode into town in February 1877 its peacekeeping record, or what was left of it, was an object of wide ridicule. When he left, almost a decade later, the reputation of its police force was wholesomely respected.

In Belleville, the routine administration of the law started running downhill with the dismissal in late 1876 of the town's police chief. No one could agree on a new appointee and — to compound the issue — the former incumbent refused to quit. The argument split council, the police commission, even the bench into opposing factions and Belleville found itself with two police chiefs.

Chief Hugh McKinnon.

The situation disintegrated New Year's Eve when the Grand Trunk Railway workers struck, vowing to halt all traffic. Belleville was a terminal point and the strikers swarmed the station. The local police force, comprised by local politics, was useless. Council panicked, petitioned for troops and workers were faced in 1877 A.D. with bayonets pricking their already-aroused passions. The natural result was a shambles of rioting which brought widespread criticism. At city hall, however, the factions, long past the point of sense and dignity, fought over a chief constable's appointment.

Waxily, a fractious magistrate suspended a police sergeant for refusing to serve a warrant. The sergeant refused to be suspended. The magistrate ordered a constable to serve it. The petrified officer explained to an alderman if he did execute the document his chief, recognized by some as the official police head, would suspend him. If he didn't, on the other hand, the magistrate who recognized the opposing claimant to office, would also suspend him. In this situation there was justification for the *Intelligencer* editor who complained: "The police haven't made an arrest for a week."

Finally, one of the chief constables retaliated by charging the magistrate with "serious dereliction of duty and objectionable habits." Obviously, it could go no further. Council finally reeled to its senses and began seeking outside for a new chief.

For once, the town's hapless police committee had fallen on happy times, for in one letter was sealed the fate of local law administration for the next decade. It was an application from Hamilton, signed Hugh McKinnon.

References to Mr. McKinnon's capabilities also came from Hamilton's police chief. But the public record of the man already had gone before him. Even at that date, the name of Hugh McKinnon the law enforcer was something to conjure with.

A powerful figure of a man, he combined the nimbleness of a Scottish mind with great physical strength and endurance. The first already had won him renown as a provincial detective, the second as a heavyweight champion athlete of North America. It was a formidable character combination for a man in the police service of his time and, in any region but the Anglo-Saxon Ontario of the day, it might have made him a fabled figure. He was a walking blend of sleuth and strongman — a Pinkerton and a Wyatt Earp.

As a provincial detective working out of Caledonia he already had made his mark in the early years of Confederation. But it was his adventures with the historically-notorious Black Donnellys near Lucan that created province-wide admiration.

By 1870 that Irish immigrant family had sufficiently terrorized the Queen's peace officers and citizens in the Lucan district to merit attention from the central authorities. As its police agent in the area, the provincial government sent McKinnon to judicially gather evidence for conviction.

McKinnon not only cased the Donnellys, he lived and slept among them until he had sufficient evidence for arrest. Then he returned with warrants and took five of them into custody. The fact that his witnesses refused to testify against the hideous crew who were thus released by default, removed not a whit from his reputation.

He had become the first lawman ever to move against the Donnellys — and the way he had carried it off inspired widespread awe in a masculine society.

This then, seven years later, was the man who applied for the post as chief constable of Belleville. Why, with such a background he should do so, may need further explanation. Perhaps it was the challenge of a situation that insulted the professionalism of a man dedicated to the ideal law enforcement. Whatever the reason, the desperate town councillors snatched at his application and on February 10, 1877, the burly, heavily-moustached, champion athlete and sleuth was sworn into office. He then spent a quiet weekend surveying his new beat.

It was no easy mark at the best of times. With a demoralized, ridiculed police force it was the worst of times. It was a lusty era, when the law had trouble enough making itself respected under normal conditions. Violence was a natural resource when men differed, and it was not confined to the matching of brawn — but, often bullets. The contemporary western pioneers were not the only continentals fairly free with a gun. Belleville newspapers of the day are peppered with reports of pistol shots haphazardly fired by everyone from lunatics and irate householders and hoboes. The same newssheets reveal that Belleville also had its share of houses that were not homes. But the days of impunity were now numbered.

Down on the motley with mighty law-enforcing strides marched McKinnon — reorganizing the force, mincing down the musclemen; bustling bar-room brawlers and bawdy into the cells, giving the town its first real taste of a strong arm of the law.

By the year's end even the staid *Intelligencer* was moved to comment: "It is to be placed to the credit of the chief that he has succeeded within eleven months in making the force which was completely disorganized, thoroughly efficient; that the number of arrests was greater than in any previous year, and that the receipts from fines more than double those of any other year in the history of Belleville."

It was the type of public encomium that would be constantly reiterated during the next ten years as the chief gave good measure for salary rendered. Unfortunately at the end of that time the citizens did not match their gallant words with deeds and McKinnon's civic service was to end shabbily.

In the meantime, he continued his relentless pursuit of law enforcement. Instilling his men with a morale they had never before known, he gave them new uniforms, patterned after the New York fashion; drew up a series of strict regulations for their behavior and marshalled them as a forceful if small, disciplined body as Belleville incorporated itself as a city on Dominion Day, 1878.

Then he settled down to real, organized law enforcement. His engagements on behalf of the law ranged far and wide beyond Belleville and won him note throughout the province. Tracking thugs and tricksters operating singly or in gangs, pursuing horse-thieves and murderers, McKinnon set a relentless pace. His physical endeavours were matched with a sleuth's intelligence, so that he never moved until he had an airtight case. His methods won him conviction after conviction. Whether the challenge demanded intellectual application or sheer physical courage, nothing was too great to escape his intention — enforcing the law.

It was an era of journalism when police news provided leaven from the heavy political and social crusades of the news columns. And Ontario readers regularly digested the adventures of Belleville's police chief. The names mean nothing now, but they caused wide attention then. Subscribers read of McKinnon's revelations of the sensational Prince Edward County murder of a man called Lazier and how McKinnon single-handed brought two men to justice for the crime; how McKinnon matched brains and brawn with "the famous Zufelt gang" eventually cornering the thugs. The scouring went on for almost a decade until 1888.

McKinnon's last year in the city's service opened in typically zestful fashion, filled with encounters — and one last heroic gesture that nearly cost him his life.

A newspaperman's dream as much as a criminal's nightmare, The Chief kept the presses humming with good copy almost immediately after the New Year's bells stopped peeling.

January 4th he was revealing his unravelling of an arson conspiracy in which he had arrested a couple named Pell. January

13th, local readers waded through the details of a determined police assault on brothel activities "in that crib of iniquity on Zwick's Island". January 18th the reading was even hotter as the *Intelligencer* trumpeted: "A Social Scandal — Bride of a few hours robbed of her treasure." The robber was McKinnon and the treasure a bigamous wretch from out of town of course — whose assaults on local virtue had been promptly uncovered by The Chief. So it continued for most of the year. McKinnon hunting down horse-thieves; McKinnon leading his men against a gang of railroad robbers; McKinnon taking time out to arrest a drunk; McKinnon facing down a crazed armed man after a shooting spree in the city's north end.

But of all of the story-making exploits, the one which likely gave him most satisfaction before relinquishing his Belleville command, was what the out-of-town press termed "the Chief's adventures with the notorious Coffin McDonald."

Alexander McDonald, to give his natal name, had one more claim to fame besides being a native of Thurlow township. From the newssheets of the day he emerges as one of the most delightful rogues in Ontario history. An engaging cheat, lier and robber, he was a veritable Scarlet Pimpernel. He could fleece a lawyer as suavely as a bumpkin, pause long enough to steal a horse, trade it for cash, then disappear into thin air.

He delighted in having the last laugh. Once, he appeared in a Belleville court for sentence immaculately attired, then created a sensation when a spectator recognized McDonald's suit as his own wedding clothes, stolen the night before his marriage months before.

On another occasion McDonald nipped over the walls of Hastings county jail and disappeared into the county. He paused long enough to purloin a batch of chickens owned by a county constable hunting him — then left enough evidence so the officer would know who had called. On top of all this — to add insult to public wrath — he claimed family ties with his namesake John A. Macdonald, the Prime Minister himself!

Since he was a native of Thurlow, sooner or later he crossed swords with McKinnon. In the early rounds of the duel, the sleuth pinioned his adversary and at last, it seemed to the people of Ontario, McDonald had met his match. But McKinnon's initial triumph was short-lived.

McDonald, up before the assizes turned in a virtuoso performance depicting himself as an unfortunate, victimized by drink. The judge, apparently much affected, ordered the supreme chancer to the local jail for one month — hoping he would see the error of his ways.

McKinnon seethed at his opponent who — to quote the *Intelligencer* — "called divine blessings upon the judge's head as he was being led from the prisoner's dock." In no time flat, the irrepressible McDonald slipped quietly over the jail wall and the duel was on again.

McKinnon the detective, however, finally figured the fatal flaw in his opponent's character. The gay trickster, while a classic rogue, was a scrupulous family man. He was dearly attached to his wife and could not abide his roving career without the odd trip home. McKinnon kept all points alerted and eventually received a dividend. Someone resembling McDonald was seen near Shannonville. In dead of night, the chief assembled a party of men and struck out for the home in Thurlow. There was a brief woodland chase, gunfire by a nervy policeman, and the game was in the bag.

McKinnon hailed his quarry before the bench and this time had the satisfaction of seeing him get seven years — in the maximum security of Kingston penitentiary.

It was The Chief's last big investigation in Belleville, but not his last adventure.

The year 1886 had been a catastrophic one for fires in the Quinte district, with Belleville among the hardest hit. In the early hours of an October morning the fire bells tolled again and the brigades turned out — this time to the Dafoe House, Belleville's biggest hostelry and one of Canada's leading provincial hotels.

Its destruction was at once obvious and firemen concentrated on rescuing the inmates. Among them were the The Chief and his aging mother.

The *Intelligencer* recounts what happened next: "The Chief turned back to rescue his aged mother, who had passed her eightieth year. He became confused and on approaching a stairway which led to safety turned away, thinking that he must be going into the hottest of the fire. At this critical moment when he had turned away from the only avenue of safety and was feeling effects of dense smoke, he was found by officer Patrick Hayes, who was hunting for him, and taken into safety . . . Mrs. McKinnon was rescued by being taken from her room window."

Two weeks later the *Intelligencer* had reason to mention The Chief again, this time in a cryptic one-line statement: "Chief

McKinnon is a candidate for the Chieftanship of the Hamilton Police." One morning shortly after, a glum constable confirmed the end of the McKinnon reign in Belleville when he told a police reporter: "Well he's going to Hamilton, and I don't know whether I'm sorry or glad." The sense of loss was common to the city. McKinnon was a prize possession who had become an institution and a fount of civic pride.

However, the association between man and community ended meanly. The police commission, in tribute to their famous servant's services decided to give a bonus of seventy-five dollars — one month's extra pay. When the bill came before city council an argument ensued. Echoing singular, if familiar, sentiments, one alderman was quoted as declaring "while he believed the chief was entitled to every consideration from the citizens of Belleville for his performance of duty, he was opposed to voting away public money."

The grubbiness of the wrangle ended in embarrassment as McKinnon rose and declined the gratuity since "any opposition to the granting of it robbed the gift of the pleasure that would accompany it."

Then McKinnon, headed for even greater things and a more appreciated career, went back to Hamilton from whence he had come ten years before.

Belleville's First Tragedy

The first murder recorded in the criminal annals of Belleville took place in October, 1835, in front of what was known as Hambly's. The parties to it were a man named John Watson and another named William Caldwell. The murder arose out of a horse trade. Watson was a gunsmith and at one time owned a lot of property in town, and a farm in the country. His wife was then living, and he had two children, a boy and a girl. Watson's son traded a horse with Caldwell, and the latter got the best of the bargain. The trade is said to have taken place about two months before the murder was committed.

On the afternoon when the murder occurred, Caldwell and Watson, the younger had a quarrel about the trade, and the elder Watson was also present. The latter took his son's part, and then Caldwell clinched with him. Watson stepped back drew a dagger from an inner pocket, and stabbed Caldwell through the abdomen, the blade going through the body and the point showing through the back. When the dagger was drawn from Caldwell's body, there was not a drop of blood on it. The place in front of which the tragedy took place was a tavern and the victim walked in there unassisted and died in a short time. Watson walked into a boot and shoe store next door and was arrested there.

A preliminary hearing of the case followed before Captain Baldwin and Squire Marshall, and the prisoner was committed for trial and taken to Kingston. The trial resulted in the conviction of Watson and he was condemned to be hanged. The execution took place in the following summer. The son was a witness of the event.

Public hanging.

Former Executions

The first hanging which occurred in Belleville was that of T. Barnhardt, a halfbreed, who was executed during the summer of 1854. He came to this country during its early settlement and squatted on a piece of land in Tyendinaga township, which he partially cleared and claimed as his own. A gentleman named Dafoe, father of Daniel McCarthy Dafoe, Esq., purchased the land in question, and proceeded with the sheriff to eject Barnhardt, who threatened to shoot Mr. Dafoe if he attempted to get possession of his land. When the sheriff and Mr. Dafoe proceeded towards the squatter's cabin, Barnhardt stepped to the door with rifle in hand and ordered them off or he would shoot. Advancing another step after the threat was made, Mr. Dafoe was shot dead, the bullet penetrating his heart. The murderer was tried and convicted. Mr. Geo. E. Henderson, Q.C. defended the accused, the defence set up being that of insanity. Judge McLean presided and when he pronounced the sentence he was deeply moved, the condemned man having been an old and trusted servant in his family. Judge Gywnne was the crown prosecutor on the occasion.

The second execution was that of Samuel Peter Rock, who suffered death for the murder of a man named Robert Dickie, a settler on the Hastings road, in Monteagle township. The deed was committed on the 11th of January, 1859, and the execution took place on the 12th of June of the same year. The particulars of this horrible murder are as follows: Mr. Dickie, on the day of the murder, entered his house after a short absence and found that a box containing papers and money to the amount of one hundred dollars had been broken open, the papers scattered about the floor and the money missing. Dickie mentioned the circumstances to a lad named Barbeau, who had entered the house with him. Opening a door leading into an adjoining room, Dickie observed Rock, who was in his employment, standing in one corner of the room with a gun in his hand which, upon the door being opened, he immediately raised and fired, the ball taking effect in Dickie's head, killing him instantly. The murderer also attempted to shoot the boy but he escaped. Rock took to the woods but was soon captured, tried, convicted and executed as above stated.

A Tragic Couple who gave Belleville a Gallows Party

by Harry Mulhall

The mid-century migration of Victorian settlers to the greener pastures of Upper Canada had many an anguished personal sequel.

But, in the annals of the era, none was more dramatically tragic than the brief New World chronicle of Richard and Mary Aylward. Seeking peace and plenty, they died in violent public ignominy in Belleville a century ago. Yet today, the shame of their end rests not so much with them as their times.

Convicted of murder, they were hanged side by side before thousands of their fellows, many of them blind drunk, all of them victims of mass morbidity. As seen by contemporary reporters, their short existence in Canada and their macabre deaths now reveals a rounded social cameo of their environment.

Central figure of the grim episode is Mary Aylward. It was by her hand that she and her husband came to the public gallows. At first a figure of public outrage, she evoked such compassion when she died at twenty-three leaving three infant orphans, that one newspaper was moved to laud her "noble conduct." It was she who set down the prelude of the bleak tale, writing from her cell in Hastings County jail on the eve of execution.

The story began in the Ireland of the Black Forties — its nation reduced to a desperate remnant by famine, where each blighted potato crop reaped a new harvest of hatred for an Imperial landlord.

Mary O'Brien was born at Arpatrick, County Limerick, her childhood spanning that disastrous decade. In 1852, then twelve years old, she and a brother joined the great trans-Atlantic flight of her countrymen and immigrated to a sister in Connecticut.

Four years later she married Richard Aylward and, in 1856, the young couple crossed the border and took up residence with his aunt near Guelph. The same year they moved northeast through

Upper Canada, or Canada West as it had been designated, and settled near Kaladar. In 1861 they finally shifted to the "unfortunate place" — the northern townships of Hastings County. They began breaking land on the Wicklow-Monteagle township line where land grants had attracted other hopeful pioneers. Their immediate neighbour — divided by a two-acre field — was the family of William Munro, who had arrived two months earlier.

At first all went well and life among the settlers — linked in common endurance — was cordial along the line. Gradually, however, it seems the bleak hardships endemic in their way of life and the bitter personal backgrounds of many immigrants, manifested itself in human relations. And the Aylwards appeared at the centre of it. Bickering broke out, violent threats were made, mischief-making and quarrels ensued.

Mary Aylward charges one incident when, two days after her confinement with child, three neighbouring settlers broke into their shack, beat up her husband and kicked her in the stomach.

The situation apparently was not helped any by malicious gossip which, at one point, she believed accused her of abnormal relationships with her husband.

Before her death she felt compelled to deny in a published letter "the calumnious fabrication, namely that my dear husband and I were brother and sister."

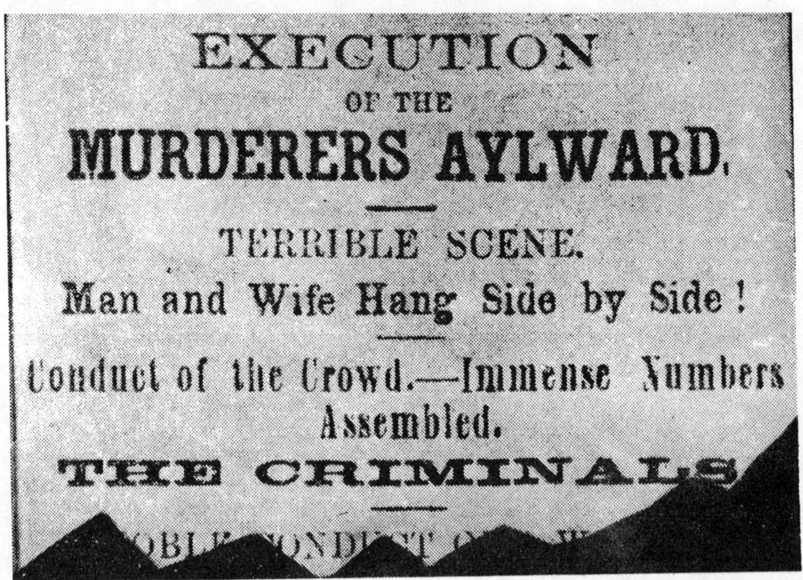

The closer the neighbour, the more temperamental the situation, it appears, and a grave breach developed between the Munros and the Aylwards. It finally came to a head over allegations by Aylward that Munro's hens were trespassing in his grainfields.

Early in May, when there was still snow on the ground and nothing to be cut, the Aylwards appeared at a neighbour's to sharpen a scythe. The fact, it had been earlier borrowed from Munro, was tragic irony, as events a week later proved. The fatal incident in the whole disarray of neighbourhood acrimony occurred May 16, 1862. It went like this:

An argument developed over Munro's hens again filching Aylward's grain. Aylward ordered off Munro and his son at shotgun point. Munro grabbed his gun; Aylward snatched a double-barrelled pistol from his bosom — only to have it knocked to the ground. Young Munro stooped to pick it up. Aylward fired the shotgun in his direction. He was wounded painfully, but not seriously. The young settler's wife stepped in. Snatching up the scythe Mary Aylward dashed from the house and felled the elder Munro with a blow. The action turned a sufficiently serious altercation to a deadly tragedy.

Viciously slashed about the shoulder and head, Munro dragged himself home across the field, took to his bed — and died twelve days later. While the incident provoked consternation in the settlement, no action was taken immediately. Feeling against the Aylwards ran high in the pioneer community, but it was not until Munro's death that the formal processes of society bestirred themselves.

At first the young Irish couple were not fearful of any consequences. Testimony at their trial in Belleville quoted a boastful Mary Aylward describing to her neighbours the results of the affray, calling on God Almighty to increase the elder Munro's pain. Her husband, she said, had shot the son and "If he is not dead, I hope he is." The Irishness of that sally was to help pin a gallows together. Yet even the victim himself apparently demurred in taking any action against the couple, as suggested by a neighbour at Mundo's deathbed. "When I said the parties ought to be arrested he (Monro) said he had no business interfering with them." John Rouse, the lone defence witness, testified at the trial.

Some twelve days later news of the settler's death raced through the township. That day Andrew Jelly, reeve of Tudor township, gathered a party of neighbours and arrested Mrs. Aylward. Two days later she was formally arrested with her husband by crown officers, both of them were charged with murder and escorted to the county jail at Belleville.

Their incarceration created a sensation in the county, agog for details, impatient for the trial — anticipating its conclusion. For if justice weighed the scales against the accused it would mean a double hanging to be witnessed. And such it proved — although the public had to patiently bide its time to fall when the Assizes would sit.

The opening of the sessions, however, had a preliminary shock in store for the public — and an ominous prelude for the Aylwards. Immediately preceding their trial, in the first week of the Assizes, a Belleville man named Morris Moorman went before Chief Justice William B. Draper, charged with the fatal stabbing of a local citizen, L. Wentworth Taylor. Despite His Lordship's parting remarks that there were no excusable grounds for the incident, the jury within a half-hour returned a verdict of not guilty.

Reported the *Hastings Chronicle:* "His Lordship appeared so startled by the verdict that he was unable to utter a word and simply discharged the prisoner." The Chronicle followed up with an angry editorial denouncing the Moorman verdict as "inexplicable, misguided and erroneous." "We feel that it will operate injuriously upon the best interests of society and that is the reason we feel called upon to make these observations," was its outraged conclusion. "After such verdicts life cannot be considered so sacred or so secure a thing as it was before." It was in this environment that the jury was chosen and sworn October 20 to decide the next matter on the docket — the sensational Aylward murder case.

Yet, the young immigrants caused a favourable stir as they appeared publicly for the first time, to hear their case argued between Adam Wilson, solicitor-general for Canada West, and defence counsel James O'Reilly, assisted by John Finn. Says the *Chronicle:* "The appearance of the prisoners in the dock created a sensation and prepossessed those present strongly in their favour — but as the honourable Solicitor General unravelled link after link in their chain of guilt, this feeling gave way and one of horror at the manner in which they compassed the death of Munro took its place."

And little wonder. For the prosecution with irrefutable deftness, built fact on fact to claim that the slaying was not, after all, the result of a fatal pique and momentary loss of emotional control, but a conspiracy. Remarks made before and after the incident by both Aylwards took on a new significance as the Crown assembled a succession of witnesses before the jury. Most damning of all was the statement by a neighbour that the Aylwards had come to her house a week before to have their scythe sharpened.

Faced with this, James O'Reilly nonetheless made an impassioned appeal for Aylward to be freed and his wife convicted on a reduced charge of manslaughter — alleging the act being the consequences of a wife blindly aiding her husband in trouble. Mr. O'Reilly spoke for ninety minutes, defending the actions and statements of the Aylwards as consequences of provoked anger; their sharpening of the scythe as a normal practice for farmers approaching harvest season.

That implement — by its absence — imparted a touch of grisly humour to the trial. A shame-faced law officer, W. E. D. Eadus, who arrested the couple, admitted they had willingly surrendered both the scythe and Alyward's shotgun to his safekeeping. On the journey to Belleville jail "the scythe and gun were placed at the door of the tavern where we were staying and in about a minute afterwards on returning to look for them — the scythe was not there." The embarrassed Eadus posted a reward seeking its return — but it never was seen again. Absence of the murder weapon, however, was no more profit to the defence than its other propositions.

Judge Draper quickly demolished the manslaughter claims of the defence and singled out the sharpening of Munro's own scythe by Mrs. Aylward as "fearful testimony." ". . . take this woman's whole conduct through the whole case and we find nothing but the most cold-blooded barbarity," he said.

It took the jury two hours to reach a verdict. It was guilty — for both accused — but with a strong recommendation of mercy.

His Lordship acknowledged the recommendation but warned the condemned: "I can hold out to you no hope of mercy in this world; seek therefore from the God you have offended that mercy which man refuses to you in this." He followed the chilling admonition with the death sentence — and, says the *Chronicle*, he "was much affected" as he intoned the sentence of death by public hanging on December 8.

"You may hang away," shouted Alyward. "I'm not guilty." "Yes. They may hang away," his wife rejoined defiantly. "We're innocent." As they were being led away the couple "spoke to one another and laughed in an unfeeling manner," noted the *Chronicle* reporter.

However, not all dismissed them to their gloomy end so righteously and the drama had another act to run before its gruesome finale. Lodged in separate cells, the couple intermittently received visitors — among them lawyer John Finn.

If Finn had lost the case in the judicial arena he at least had drawn a hopeful concession from twelve of the Aylward's peers that society might not exact its legal due. Apparently, he was not alone. Armed with the recommendation for mercy he set about organizing a petition to the Governor General, and found enough support-at-large to present three such appeals before December 8.

However, as the execution date neared and no decision was received of clemency, the *Chronicle* felt constrained to point out the folly of raising false hopes. The evidence, it said, had not been impeached nor questioned in "any of its shocking details." Were the petitioners willing to abrogate abolition of capital punishment? "The security and safety of a society so intimately depends up the swiftness and the certainty of the punishment of the guilty that every man incurs a grave responsibility when he allows the kindness of his heart to influence him to prevent that punishment from being inflicted upon anyone whose guilt is beyond doubt." ". . . it becomes our painful duty to point out that the interests of society are above the promptings of generous impulse toward condemned felons, and that without the infliction of exemplary punishments in all cases, the safeguards of life and property will be endangered, if not entirely destroyed."

Despite Finn's gallant exertions, the Executive Council was of the same opinion and shortly before the date set by Judge Draper it became known there would be no commutation. The public hanging, side by side of the young backwood parents would take place as originally scheduled!

In her cell Mary Aylward, now reconciled to death, asked for pen and paper and, for the record, set forth her version of the fatal affray. "I protest before God and man that the unfortunate blow I struck in defence of my husband on my own soil and near my own home, among my own helpless children. I say in my lonely cell and on the brink of the grave, that I had not the least thought of killing Munro, that I did not premeditate the unfortunate blow . . ."

Then, in a second note, moving in its simple eloquence, she set down her last admonitions to her three young children: "God has willed it that your Pa and Ma will suffer death on Monday next. I hope He will have mercy on our souls. My wish is that when you, my dear infant children, will come to the use of reason, that you will pray to the Almighty God for the repose of the souls of your Pa and Ma, who loved you dearly . . ." With Irish fretfulness she added: "My sincere wish and command is that my children will be brought up in the Catholic religion — the church of their fathers."

By December 8 Belleville was settling down to expectations of Christmas. The weather had the fitting seasonal edge to it. The night before the thermometer had dropped to five below zero and the morning was bitter cold.

Belleville Court House and Gaol.

Nonetheless, business was brisk — for thousands of outsiders were bustling into the county town. They were to play that ancient and integral role in the final ritual of capital punishment — the gallows mob. The contemporary report from the *Chronicle* describes it best. All that is lacking is the exact location of the hanging ground, authority for which seems to have been lost with time. "From an early hour in the morning, and even the day before, large sleigh loads of people were seen wending their way to town to witness the execution . . . and the streets were thronged with men and women hastening to the place of execution. By ten o'clock there could not have been less than five thousand on the ground, one fourth of whom were women . . . some of whom we are informed, had travelled in the night from sixty to seventy-five miles and were on the ground by daybreak and did not leave it, notwithstanding the intense cold, until 12 o'clock when the final and awful scene closed.

"In the immense crowd we saw numerous instances of young men drunk and unable to stand without assistance! and, quarrelling, hooting and yelling, combined to make it one of the most terrible and heart-rending scenes we ever witnessed. And we cannot but pause and ask what good effects arise from these disgusting public executions. Do they not rather pander to the vitiated taste of low morals, than act as warnings to others? If a fellow creature has really forfeited his life, and the law deems it necessary to execute him as an example to evil doers, would not every purpose be answered by a private execution, at which only a limited number of persons were present — the officials of the County etc. . . ."

The Aylwards had been kept in separate cells since their condemnation and had not seen each other since. Their final parting before the gallows was tersely described by an eyewitness as "affecting in extreme." Accompanied by two local priests, Fathers Lawlor and Brennan, they were conducted to scaffold where they joined in the responses of the Catholic liturgy for the dying.

"After the prayers were over," said the *Chronicle*, "and the rope adjusted, the male prisoner attempted to address the people present but was overcome by emotion and stopped. The couple then joined the priests in the Lord's Prayer and the bolt was drawn."

And so the gruesome predicament of the young immigrants snapped to an end — at least within minutes. Attending physicians proclaimed Mary Aylward dead in ninety seconds. It took her husband another full minute to give up the ghost.

What had taken hours of chilled patience to witness was over quickly. The crowd started drifting away — although there was still something for the morbid to watch. "The bodies," reported the *Chronicle*, "were allowed to remain suspended for about thirty-five minutes — when they were taken down and delivered into the care of their friends. They were buried in the Catholic cemetery in the afternoon at three o'clock and the fearful tragedy closed — we are afraid, without benefitting by example a solitary person present except inasmuch as it pandered to a morbid curiosity."

A crucial footnote to such journalistic loathing was written a few years later. The example was set in London, when prompted by a Royal Commission reviewing the entire process Westminster finally abolished public execution in 1868.

Early Editor
Escaped Hanging

Belleville's first newspaperman and 1841 mayor was once sentenced to be hanged for armed robbery.

In 1837, while Alexander Oliphant Petrie was running a ferry from Belleville to Rossmore on government contract, a rival set a ferry in competition. Petrie met the rival on the lower bridge, drew a pistol and demanded the money his rival had made from the illegal operation. The rival retired with Petrie to a nearby tavern to discuss the issue. The outcome: Petrie was arrested, tried and sentenced to be hanged for armed robbery.

The Kingston Gazette, which had employed Petrie about 1809 as its Belleville correspondent, remarked that the sentence "seemed severe." The sentence was never carried out and Petrie, the convicted felon, won the mayoralty race of 1841.

Belleville Sends Courier on Foot to Toronto

by Nick and Helma Mika

In April, 1924, the seventeen-year-old Belleville High School student, Cadet W. Allan Dempsey, went as courier, on foot after the manner of the old pioneers, from Belleville to Toronto. He was to deliver an invitation from Belleville Mayor W. C. Mikel to the Mayor and members of Toronto City Council; the Premier of Ontario, the Hon. G. Howard Ferguson, and members of his Cabinet; and to the acting Lieutenant-Governor Chief Justice Sir William Mulock, to attend the celebrations of the one hundred and fortieth anniversary of the settlement of Upper Canada by United Empire Loyalists to be held in Belleville the week commencing June 16, 1924. Cadet Dempsey also carried invitations for the mayors of cities and towns, the reeves of villages, and the council members of the municipalities through which he was to pass on his way to the provincial capital.

The Dempseys were United Empire Loyalists of Irish origin. Allan's ancestors, who after the close of the American Revolution came to Canada to settle, had been for four generations farmers in Prince Edward County, and Allan Dempsey still resides there today. His great-grandfather, William Dempsey, at the age of twelve, drove a team between the Carrying Place and York (Toronto) in the War of 1812, and during the 1837 Rebellion, as a captain, he marched a company of soldiers over the same route.

Allan himself, at seventeen, was a champion walker, having won the annual walking contest at the Belleville High School Field Day for three consecutive years.

He started out for Toronto on Monday, April 21, leaving Belleville at twenty minutes after nine in the morning. Dressed smartly in his cadet uniform and Glengarry cap and wearing sturdy boots, he carried a tin box containing the official invitations, and souvenir post cards which he was to distribute along the way.

By noon he had covered sixteen miles and arrived in Trenton, where he was a guest of the Rotory Club for dinner. Tired and foot-sore, but in excellent spirit, he made it to Brighton the first day and stayed overnight there with friends.

Cadet W. Allan Dempsey presenting invitation to Mayor of Toronto, W. W. Hiltz.

He left Brighton on Tuesday afternoon and walked eight miles to Colborne, where he visited a former Prince Edward County family. The next morning he left bright and early and reached Cobourg shortly after noon. After dinner and a short rest he continued to Port Hope, where the Mayor invited him to dinner at a local hotel. Wherever he went, the young Belleville courier was warmly welcomed and received splendid treatment. Everywhere local newspapers carried his story and publicized the forthcoming U.E.L. celebrations to be staged in Belleville that summer. In Whitby, where Allan arrived on Friday evening, April 25, the reporter wrote:

> *Having all the appearance of a clean-living Canadian youth, clear of eye, and the picture of health, Cadet Dempsey appealed to one as a worthy descendant of that noble band of hardy pioneers who settled in Canada following the American war of Independence. And he comes of real U.E.L. stock, and it is fitting that he should be chosen to carry the credentials he does in the old-time manner of courier.*

Part of Allan's duties was to obtain from the mayor and the chief of police at each place through which he passed a signature on his credential sheet, to prove he had been there.

On Saturday evening, April 26, 1924, Allan arrived in Toronto. The next day he presented the invitation to the Premier of Ontario. Alderman W. H. Patterson wired from Toronto to Belleville on Monday morning:

> *W. H. Ireland (M.P.P.) and myself introduced Courier Dempsey to Premier yesterday. Looking fine. Being entertained by Toronto City Entertainment Committee.*

His Worship Mayor W. W. Hiltz of Toronto received Allan at City Hall at one p.m., Monday, April 28. Being of United Empire Loyalist stock himself, the mayor expressed his pleasure at the invitation and promised to be present at the celebrations in Belleville together with a number of his council members, if nothing unforeseen happened.

Having his duties as U.E.L. courier completed, Allan returned to Belleville by train. He was met at the station by Mayor Mikel of Belleville, Mayor Blakely of Trenton, several Aldermen and other city officials.

Allan brought with him a letter from Mayor Hiltz, addressed to Mayor W. C. Mikel, which read in part, ". . . If Cadet Dempsey is a sample of the boys you have in Belleville and the Belleville High School, your city has reason to be proud of your young men."

Belleville Macs Skyrocket to World Acclaim

by Nick and Helma Mika

This is the story of an event that made Belleville famous not only in Ontario but in all of Canada and even across Europe. It is the story of a great hockey team, and the story of the team's manager whose enthusiasm and devotion to hockey cost him his well-paid job. The team which made Belleville for a while the most colourful place in the country were the "Belleville Macs" or, as they were officially known, the "Belleville McFarlands".

The exciting story of this world-famous hockey team began in the fall of 1956 and ended on November 6th, three years later, when a Royal Commission found that the City of Belleville had acted in "gross negligence" by allowing $110,000 of taxpayers' money to be spent to finance a hockey team.

During these three years the Belleville Macs left a brief but blazing trail in the city's sports history. During this period the Belleville McFarlands were born, won Canadian and World Hockey Championships, ignited a judicial inquiry and faded into oblivion as a team, if not as Belleville's greatest hockey heros.

This story could only have happened in Canada, where hockey enthusiasm and the obsession to produce the best hockey players in the world might well prevail over reason. When the Macs had caught on fire and defeated team after team, when the desire to beat the last opponent and win the World Championship had gripped the Macs' boosters and supporters, when Bellevillians shouted: "Go, Macs, go!" and the hockey fever bordered on hysteria, anything was possible. Nobody asked, "how are we going to pay for this?"

It all started innocently enough in the fall of 1956. That year City Council decided to sponsor a hockey team of the Senior "A" league in the eastern division of the Ontario Hockey Association. Prior to this Belleville had sponsored a team in the "B" category and had lost about $6,000 in the deal. To make the new project financially feasible, Belleville Mayor Gerald Hyde and some of the City Councillors approached Mr. Harvey McFarland, a prominent businessman and Mayor of the Town of Picton, to sponsor the team. Mr. McFarland agreed to contribute $3,000, no strings attached. The delighted promoters responded by naming the team the "Belleville McFarlands".

At that time Harvey McFarland had little personal interest in hockey. As far as he was concerned, the Belleville club consisted of a few youngsters eager to play hockey and he was willing to assist.

Managed by Drury Denyes, the club finished atop the Eastern League standing with a record of twenty-nine wins, three ties and twenty defeats. This outstanding record was attributed to the guidance of the new player-coach, Ike Hildebrand.

Belleville oldtimers, 1904.

The Belleville McFarlands consisted of goalie Gordie Bell, Keith MacDonald, Minnie Menard, Floyd Crawford, Moe Benoit, Lionel Botley, "Bep" Guidolin, Russ Kowalchuk, Joe Lepine, Gerry Goyer, Keith Montgomery, Dave Jones, Eddie Marineau, Jean-Paul Payette, "Wiener" Brown, Barton Bradley, and Johnny Muretich.

The strongest opponents the Macs encountered in the early days of their spectacular career were the powerful Kitchener-Waterloo Dutchmen. By this time tickets for the Macs' home games were next to impossible to get, and the Belleville arena which holds 2,500 was jammed with well over 3,000 spectators who went wild as the Macs beat the Dutchmen five to four in the series' opener. The swelling ranks of supporters of the Macs accompanied them to their out-of-town games to cheer them on and keep them winning.

But despite excellent attendance figures at the games, red ink was beginning to show on the books. Nobody paid attention to it, only the manager, Drury Denyes, occasionally felt uneasy.

A series of circumstances eventually lead to the inevitable catastrophic end. In previous years the city's cheques had been signed by both the city manager and the city treasurer. During Gerald Hyde's administration the positions of city manager and treasurer had been combined, and Drury Denyes held the new post; he also was manager of the Belleville Macs. During his tenure of office municipal cheques were thus not counter-signed, as required by the Ontario Municipal Act, but neither council nor the bank raised objections.

In the meantime the Macs went from victory to victory. All their opponents were wiped out. The cry then was "On to Kelowna, B.C. and the Allan Cup!"

The Belleville Memorial Arena Commission informed Mr. McFarland that it could only pay for the trip out West, but not for the players' salaries. The Mayor of Picton agreed to take care of the payroll.

The Macs won the first game four to one in Kelowna, but the "Apple Kings" beat the Macs in the second, third and fourth games, and the Ontario team was on the verge of being eliminated.

On Monday, April 28, 1958 the tide turned and the Macs, through sheer determination, made one of the greatest comebacks which gave Belleville its first Allan Cup Champions in the City's history.

Manager Drury Denyes with Allan Cup, 1958.

On May 6th, the Macs arrived back in Belleville. The station was dressed in its most festive garb. Never in living memory had Front Street been thronged with so many happy, celebrating citizens. Fifty thousand people turned out to welcome the Macs back home. All along the street they stood, ten deep, cheering, shouting and waving as the motorcade passed slowly by. Mounted high on the trailer of one of Mayor McFarland's long diesel trucks stood the coveted Allan Cup, the trophy which had inspired the Macs to victory.

Amid the jubilant celebrations plans were already being made to send the Macs to Prague, Czechoslovakia. Signs and posters everywhere urged people to contribute toward the $50,000 required for the trip overseas.

At the Market Square, where a massed throng of people stood shoulder to shoulder, filling every available space, Mayor Harvey J. McFarland said: "This is the proudest moment of my life! The Macs are a wonderful bunch of boys, who showed true championship. I want to especially thank the City of Belleville, its fine people, Mayor Gerry Hyde and Manager Drury Denyes. When the Macs go to Europe, I will be along to hope and pray for their success."

The Macs' Manager, Drury Denyes, at that moment, was the hero of the city and was hailed as much as the Macs themselves. The Macs' Booster Club president, Dick Beare, expressed "happiness, pride and gratitude" to him.

Looking into all the smiling faces around him, Drury Denyes, however, could not help but think about the city's hockey deficit which by now had edged over the $75,000 mark. If he were to bring the matter before City Council now, he might be forgiven in the atmosphere of excitement and enthusiasm for having spent the money to bring home the Allan Cup. Or he might lose his job over it . . . and what about the Macs? Who would defend Canada as hockey champion of the world? Perhaps the European trip would bring a profit reducing or wiping out the deficit . . .

This was a hope, reality was to be different.

The Macs were ready to go to Europe with a sole, collective purpose — to retain the World Amateur Hockey Championship for Canada. Harvey McFarland again assisted with generous donations. Jim Matthews, then the president of the team's "Booster Club", launched a fund-raising drive to help defray expenses. In all, about $50,000 were raised, and in February, 1959 the "Belleville McFarlands" invaded Europe.

Overseas, the Macs did their city and their country proud. In the preliminary round they defeated Poland, Switzerland and Czechoslovakia.

Then came the final round. The big game against Russia! Previously, the Macs had defeated Finland, Sweden and the United States. Tension mounted at home as thousands sat glued to their radios. When the game was over, Canada's team from the City of Belleville had defeated the Russians three to one.

Drury Denyes later said, "That night when Canada's flag went up and Russia's went down, I stood and watched with my heart in my mouth. At that moment I figured it had all been worth it."

At home, after one of the greatest celebrations the city ever staged, the storm broke. In May, 1959, the city auditor informed Mayor Hyde that the deficit in the account of the community rink amounted to about $110,000. Drury Denyes resigned as City Manager.

Subsequent investigations by a Royal Commission confirmed that not a penny of this staggering deficit had gone into the pocket of any individual. Mayor Harvey McFarland of Picton said to the judicial inquiry looking into the city's finances: "No Canadian ambassador can go behind the Iron Curtain and do the job of cementing public relations like a good Canadian hockey team". Keith MacDonald, the playing manager, expressed his feelings thus: "The City of Belleville has gained more than it is going to cost".

Today we see what he meant.

THE WEATHER
Tuesday — Clear and colder
Low 15, high 32.

TEMPERATURES
　　　　　　Max.　Min.
Today　　　　23　　30
One year ago　35　　25

The Ontario Intelligencer

Authorized as Second Class Mail,
Post Office Department Ottawa.

BELLEVILLE, ONTARIO, MONDAY, MARCH 16, 1959

5c Per Copy, 30c Per Week

MACS WORLD CHAMPS

Southern Ontario Racked By Winds; Heavy Damage

Seven Persons Injured, 92-Mile-an-Hour Wind

By THE CANADIAN PRESS

Churches lost their steeples, banks their windows; roads were washed out and power failures darkened many areas Sunday as rain and wind battered Southern Ontario.

Seven persons were injured as the wind rose in shrieking blasts to 92 miles an hour before the storm abated and moved away toward the east.

The winds were expected to subside to 30 miles per hour in Southern Ontario today.

The seven injured were in the Stork restaurant on the Queen Elizabeth Way near Niagara Falls, when two plate glass windows blew in.

Mr. and Mrs. John Hodd of

CHICAGO (AP) — The supposedly dying winter, showing no plan, plastered the midwestern United States with wind, snow and rain storms during the weekend and swept eastward without losing much of its power.

The wild, late winter storms left thousands of persons stranded for hours. Included were nearly 350 passengers on four Chicago and North Western Railroad trains which got stuck in 12-foot snow drifts in Wisconsin. All of the trains had sufficient fuel to heat the cars and all passengers had food during their enforced layovers, ranging up to 12 hours.

The last of the stalled trains, with 150 passengers aboard, was pulled free late Sunday night

GOVT. WILL NOT DISALLOW ACT OUTLAWING IWA

Likely Issue Will Go to Supreme Court

OTTAWA (CP) — The federal government will not disallow provincial legislation outlawing the International Woodworkers of America in Newfoundland, it was learned today.

Prime Minister Diefenbaker was expected to announce this to the Commons this afternoon.

Informants said it was likely that the cabinet will refer the issue to the Supreme Court of Canada but that—at mid-morning— no final decision had been reached on this.

The cabinet has been discussing the tricky Newfoundland question for several days and sources indicated there has been a division among the ministers on what should be done about Premier Smallwood's

Czechs Acclaim Macs

By GEORGE H. CARVER
Sports Editor

PRAGUE — Canada's Red Ensign fluttered proudly in rafter-packed Zimni Stadium here Sunday and "O Canada" rang out in a paean of victory as the Belleville McFarlands were acclaimed the 1959 world hockey champions.

The proud but hockey-weary Macs were given a thunderous ovation by 15,000 happy Czechs, delirious with the wine of victory, after their national team had defeated the highly-favored Canadians. The Czechs played brilliant hockey, capitalizing on Canada's penalties and the off-goal shooting of the Macs, to chalk up their 5–3 victory.

The Czechs were a better team than the Canadians or Russians on the day's play.

A little band of Canadians, their red Mac booster tams tossed high in the air, cheered lustily as Macs' captain Floyd Crawford mounted the centre pedestal, flanked by the Russian and Czechoslovakian captains.

NASSER CHARGES BORDER ATTACK BY IRAQI TROOPS

Says Syrian Guard Wounded in Action

DAMASCUS, Syria (AP) — A new Syrian charge of Iraqi border violation added more fuel today to the burning feud between President Nasser of the United Arab Republic and Iraqi Premier Abdel Karim Kassem.

In the third such accusation in a week, a spokesman for the United Arab Republic's 1st (Syrian) Army claimed that 30 Iraqis thrust across Syria's frontier Sunday and attacked two Syrian guards, wounding one.

Lose To Czechs In Final Game But Have Goal Spread

Only Defeat Suffered By Canadians in Tourney

By ED SIMON
Canadian Press Staff Writer

PRAGUE, Czechoslovakia (CP) — The fighting Czech hockey team served notice on Canada's newly-crowned world champions Sunday that on its day it is a match for the best of international teams.

The Czechs, with virtually the same lineup that the Canadians slaughtered 7-1 in Bratislava eight days before, rang down the curtain on the tournament by springing its biggest upset when they joined Belleville 0–3 to give the champions their only defeat.

While the Canadians, who were playing their 9th game including *Robber First*

Advertising of Yesteryear

PROCLAMATION.

PIGS ! PIGS !

To His Worship the Mayor of the Town of Belleville :

WE, members of the Town Council of the Town of Belleville, beg to request you to issue a Proclamation to the inhabitants, that from and after this date all pigs found running at large in this Town will be impounded, and the By-Laws strictly enforced regarding the same.

C. G. LeVesconte,
Henry Corby,
G. Taylor,
C. L. Coleman,
James Blacklock,
James Kennedy,
M. Gillen,
L H. Henderson,
N. McArthur,
John O'Hare.

Belleville, 10th May, 1862.

NOTICE.

IN conformity with the above, notice is hereby given, that from and after the date of this Proclamation all Pigs found running at large in the Town of Belleville will be impounded, and the By-Laws strictly enforced regarding the same.

JAMES BROWN,
Mayor.

Belleville, May 10th, 1862.

LOOK THIS WAY!

BOOKS ! BOOKS ! BOOKS ! !

A LARGE ASSORTMENT, at greatly reduced prices, just opened on Front St., opposite the Globe Hotel.

GEO. I. CRONK.

Belleville, Oct. 6th, 1852. tf

TEMPERANCE.

THE friends of Temperance are invited to meet at the TEMPERANCE HALL on THURSDAY evening, the 24th instant, at 7½ o'clock, for the purpose of organizing an Open Temperance Society.

Belleville, March 23, 1870. 275,2t

SPECIAL NOTICE.

IN order to induce the public generally to witness his extraordinaay experiments,

Professor Stone

WILL

Give away to the Audience

EACH EVENING.

A large number of

BEAUTIFUL AND COSTLY PRESENTS.

March 12, 1870. 266

HOW THANKFUL WE SHOULD BE

If furnace fires would not go out,
How thankful we should be.
If living high would not give gout,
How thankful we should be.
If messenger boys were only quick,
If all our kids were never sick,
If postage stamps we need not lick,
How thankful we should be.
If taxes were not quite so steep,
How thankful we should be.
If one could go to bed and sleep.
How thankful we should be.
If monthly bills would not fall due,
If friends would stick as well as glue,
If half our plans we could get through
How thankful we should be.
If toothache were an unknown pain,
How thankful we should be,
If drunken men would not raise Cain,
How thankful we should be,
If water-pipes would never leak,
If all the deaf and dumb could speak.
If servant girls had much less cheek
How thankful we should be.
If fresh-laid eggs were never stale,
How thankful we should be.
If ships would weather every gale,
How thankful we should be.
If horses never ran away,
If boys were fond of work as play,
If donkeys would forget to bray,
How thankful we should be.
If bricks from chimneys never fell,
How thankful we should be.
If we were sure there was no hell,
How thankful we should be.
If inkstands did not get upset,
If money were not hard to get,
If we could sometimes win a bet,
How thankful we should be.

PICTURE CREDITS

Hastings County Museum, Illustrated Atlas of Hastings and Prince Edward Counties, The Intelligencer, Public Archives of Canada, Ottawa, Public Archives of Ontario, Toronto, W. A. Dempsey, Ruth Howard.

PREPARATION AND PRINTING BY THE INTELLIGENCER